"In the 1970s, I worked with the Education Department of the Museum of Modern Art (MoMA) in New York and the museum had a special exhibit by women artists. Inspired by the show, I approached museum officials and proposed an idea for a special exhibition of Deaf Art. Their response? 'Too ghettoized and not powerful enough.'

In the 1980s, MoMA had a special exhibition of African-American art. Again I approached them with the same idea. Their response? 'Too hidden and not marketable enough.'

I guess that says a lot about the dominant cultural perspective of Deaf Art. But that isn't good enough. We can't stop until Deaf Art is on par with all other forms of artistic expression. We can't stop until our art hangs next to their art and they know it is good."

— Silver

Ann Silver

ONE WAY
DEAF WAY

James W. Van Manen

empyreal  press

(art on cover)
ONE WAY, DEAF WAY | 2012

(endpapers)
UNTITLED (detail) | 1972

SILVER MOON BRAND
Copyright © 2012

Published in the United States by Empyreal Press, Seattle, Washington.

Library of Congress Control Number: 2012941723

Van Manen, James W.

    ANN SILVER: ONE WAY, DEAF WAY / James W. Van Manen
    p.   cm.
Includes bibliographic references and index.

ISBN: 978-0-9856982-0-1

1. Art, American 2. Deaf Artists—United States I. Title

First Edition

Published July 2012

From the Artist

*I dedicate this to my parents, Belle and George Silver,
who showed me the One Way.*

From the Author

*I dedicate this to my parents Marion Van Manen and
Janice and Norman Wilson, who showed me the Deaf Way.*

FOREWORD

There is no question that in the field of Deaf Studies, Deaf visual art is largely overlooked and marginalized as if it is sitting in an old chair in the back row of a bureaucratic waiting room. One might think that since it is visual, it might get recognition like a well-timed hand wave at the teacher, but unfortunately, Deaf visual art is often still ignored. There have been numerous times that I have searched in vain for historical or background information about Deaf artists and their works and often have ended up with more questions than answers.

Here are a few: I'd like to know what happened to the artwork that was displayed at the 1934 International Exhibition of Fine and Applied Arts by Deaf Artists at the Roerich Museum. When early Deaf American artists went overseas, I'd like to know with whom they studied during their time abroad. More recently, I'd like to know what impact the group *Spectrum* had on the Deaf artists who were involved in Texas in the 1970s under Betty G. Miller's leadership. How was the organization, *Deaf Artist of America* from Rochester NY created?

I want there to be a book on the historical gathering of De'VIA artists during the first Deaf Way international festival in 1989 at Gallaudet University in Washington DC. I'd love it if there were a few books that reflect on how Deaf artists create their artwork. Rough drawings or sketches included in such books might allow us to gather some insight into the artists' minds.

I believe that there is a story behind each artist's work and it must be told, and should be retold as often as possible. The more we know about Deaf artists, the more we can contribute our own creative perspectives to alter the mainstream art world's lens for a greater appreciation of Deaf Art and gain more respect for Deaf artists.

It is for these reasons that I was thrilled to hear of Jim Van Manen's bold decision to write an art biography about Ann Silver and her work. Ann Silver is well known for her signature Pop Art style. Her talent has been largely ignored for a number of years which is, to me, a crime. She is likely one of the earliest Deaf artists to openly inject her own Deafhood into artwork with a strong political message. She is one of the founders of the entire Deaf Art genre. Because of her artistic vision, people who view her artwork are often mesmerized by her controversial messages that lie underneath the popular cultural signifiers she puts on display in her work.

In one of my favorite pieces by Ann Silver, **WILL THE REAL GOYA PLEASE STAND UP?** (1996), the themes presented have brought many hours of discussion to my Deaf Art history class each year. It is one of a very few pieces that asks probing questions about what it actually means to be a Deaf artist who does Deaf Art and what this might mean or not mean to the world at large.

In this book Ann Silver's background will be discussed, but more than that, several of her pieces will be gently dissected under Van Manen's academic utility knife. They will be trimmed and revealed layer by layer so that the reader will have a full panoramic view of Silver's work in retrospective. A piece of art may stand alone simply based on its own reputation, but if we as spectators have access to the mind of the artist, the art work and the artist together may be forged into something that makes an indelible mark that will exist in the minds of many generations.

To me, that is the most unselfish contribution that anyone can offer. Van Manen may have begun this step. He mentioned to me once that a scholar

must have a passion for the artist in order to successfully write about their works. I hope that this is the start of more of this fusion-like genre of scholar-artist writers to create an infinite number of documents on other Deaf artists as well. I have to point out that his selection of Silver's work for this book truly reflects his love for the Pop Art genre of the 1960s and 1970s that greatly influences his own art work. Yes, I repeat, this author is also a talented visual artist!

I hope that you, as the reader, will find Van Manen's colorful narrative palette to Silver's works amusing as well as visually informative. More importantly, may this book start with a loud and gigantic red-yellow-blue dotted Lichtenstein-like BANG! May it bring awareness of Ann Silver's work to new generations of Deaf artists and their patrons. Ann Silver would simply love this.

Peter Cook
Storyteller, Poet & Associate Professor,
Columbia College Chicago

PREFACE

"I don't want to be known for only the work I did so long ago. I don't want to be known as *The Crayon Woman*. I have work that is languishing in my files that is as good or better than that has never seen the light of day. I have ideas for more. Why would I want to be known as *The Crayon Woman?*", said Ann Silver.

And I replied, "People choose art based on their desire, their wants. They don't choose art based on what they should want, or what is good for them to want, or what others think. Often they choose because the piece has a message for them to which they can relate. Because they relate to a piece, it becomes iconic for them. That icon is an icon of Ann Silver."

Silver cocked her head at me and laughed so I continued, "That icon they have of you may be the only way they ever access the deeper work you have done. Without the crayon icon they may never consider looking at your other work. It may become a gateway to all other things you have done. In my own life, I don't remember what piece I first saw of yours. I know I saw several and loved them. The messages were serious and you used colors and a bold style that spoke to me. I'm sitting here now because of those pieces you made—because of those icons."

"The beautiful thing is that you have so many meaningful pieces that all are different ways to say your name—Ann Silver," I told her. "So, it isn't so bad if you are *The Crayon Woman* to them for a little while, or for a long time. As all are Buddha, each piece of your work is another icon of you."

I met Ann Silver at the American Sign Language Teachers Association (ASLTA) national conference in Seattle, WA in late June 2011. She had a well-placed booth of her art in the exhibit hall. This woman, my favorite Deaf artist, was explaining her art and answering questions for anyone who walked by. It took me a few minutes to gather the courage to speak with her. It is not every day that one meets someone famous. She was selling original pieces of her work at what I considered to be bargain basement prices. She had pieces on display that had been shown in galleries and books on Deaf Art—work that was deep and somewhat controversial. She was selling many pieces that were icons of Deaf identity for at least two generations.

"Hi! I can't believe you are here! You are my favorite Deaf artist and you are here in person with all this work of yours!"

Self-effacing, she said, "Thank you! Yes, I come to a few conferences each year to sell my work. I think of myself as a conference artist in some ways."

"That's silly—you are so much more than that!" I looked at the work she had on display, the bright colors catching my eye, the iconic signs—the soup cans with real meaning, the clever play with words, the double entendre here and there... "I am proud to say that I own a copy of that one!"

Silver's brows crossed. Her head tilted. She looked at me skeptically. "Wait a minute. How do you have one of those? I have the names of nearly everyone who has bought my work."

I was a bit surprised that she felt so close to people who had mere copies of her work—or that is what I thought I had... "I bid the highest at an art auction on this piece—*ASL-ENGLISH / LINGUISTIC XING*. It is one of the prints—number 4/5."

"Oh no, they aren't prints," she said. "They are limited editions, yes, but they are not prints. Each one was hand made by me. I painted all the backgrounds, laid each one out, and placed all of the elements by hand. In many cases I added hand coloring on pieces to give them depth and make them pop. It is all hand work that I just don't have time to do anymore." What I had bid on and won several years earlier at a Deaf Art auction, thinking it was a print of a digital creation was actually a two-dimensional layered paper collage of original art with hours of personal hand crafted attention for each of five pieces similar enough to each other that she determined them to be limited editions of the same piece. I was incredulous. "Do you know that I bid twice what you are charging for that piece, in my mind thinking it was a PRINT?"

Skipping over my surprise, Silver merely nodded as if she had heard this before, "No, I did it all by hand." She tilted her head down and looked up at me with her eyes. "I am embarrassed to admit that I don't know how to use a computer. I don't have email or a website. I use a TTY to communicate with the outside world."

It took me several minutes to take in this new information. Everything I assumed I understood about this woman was untrue and deeper and more relevant than I had somehow been led to believe. Taking me away from these thoughts, she startled me.

"That means you are the one!" she said with some kind of dawning. I was perplexed and conveyed that to her. "You must be the one who bought that piece from the auction whom I didn't know. Wait a minute." She raced to a table and pulled out a paper file, neatly arranged. Silver quickly found what she was searching for. "Here it is! Come here and look." She showed me a paper bearing my signature, showing that I had taken possession of the artwork eight years prior. "I finally found you! People who are my customers are kind of like my family.

You are the long lost cousin!" What could I say to that? One of my favorite artists said I was like family... I'm sure I turned a shade or two of pink and happily smiled stupidly at her.

"You know, now you are a friend for life." She said it so quickly, nearly flippantly—her hands flying.

So I responded in similar fashion, meaning my words but cautiously I said, "But we only just met. How can you know it? How can you be so sure?"

She was sure. "When you know, you know. Get used to it. There is no getting rid of me now." And with that she laughed and hugged me, sealing the deal.

In the ensuing months, I learned much about my new friend and realized that she was quite an unsung artist. Given the changes that happened in technology she was nearly left behind in a world that moved by lighting-fast, ever present communication. Her work still spoke volumes and it needed a way to reach new audiences. I proposed that I write an art biography about her life and her work told through her art. After much thought, she cautiously agreed and *ANN SILVER: ONE WAY, DEAF WAY* is the product of nearly one year's work together.

James W. Van Manen

TABLE OF CONTENTS

Chapter 1
INTRODUCTION

"DEAF ART IS MY SOUL, MY HEART, MY CONSCIENCE"
— *Silver*

This book gives you entré into the life of an incredible woman who has done much with her life. She has traveled the world. She has met several presidents and prime ministers. She has charmed her way into situations and into places few would imagine possible for anyone. To say that she is a remarkable person is to miss the mark. While barely 20 and an undergraduate, along with a few others, she started the Deaf Art Movement. By 25 her artwork had been published in over 10 books. By 40 she had created an international symbol of sign language interpreting, and had her design work published on over 2000 book covers. By 45, after rededicating her life to studio art, she had completed over 150 pieces and defined a new art genre: Deaf Pop Art. She has taken more photographs of famous people using the ILY sign than most people can name. Once, while flying back to college following a semester

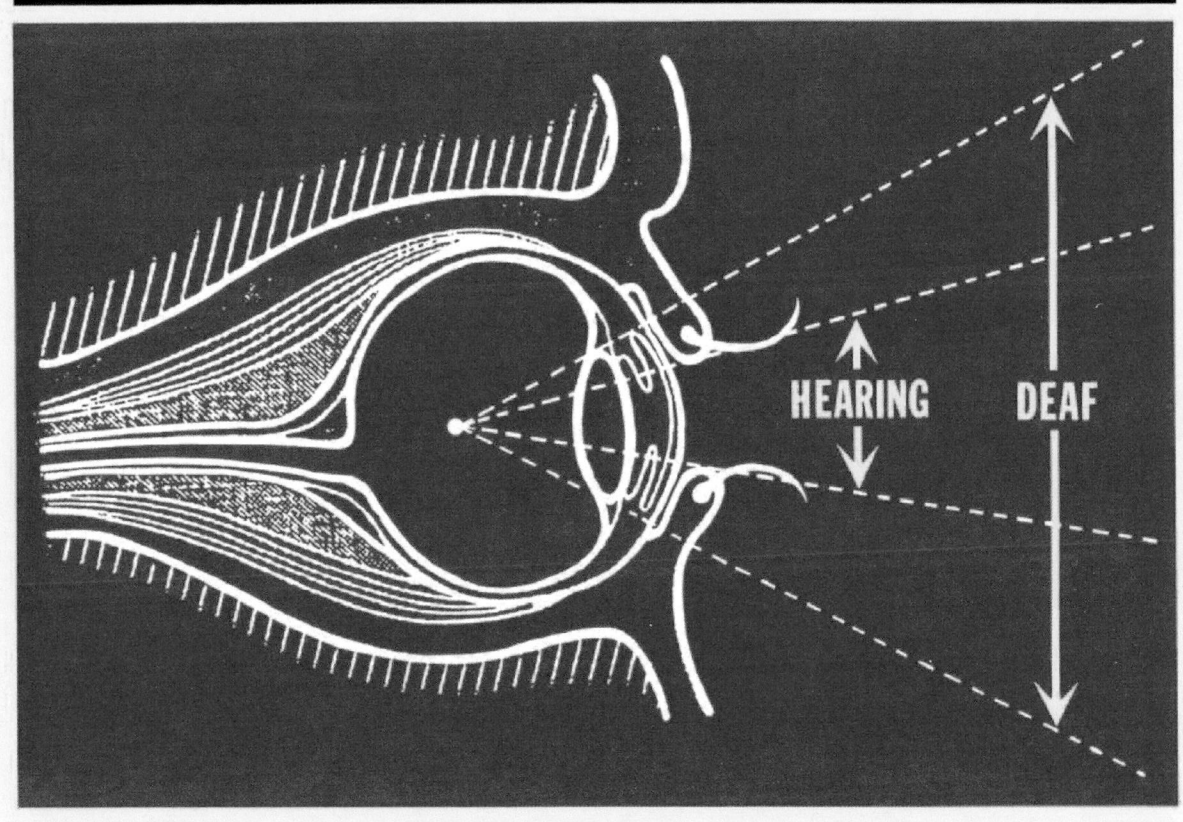

▲ The D-FACTOR THEORY No. 1 | 1996
20" x 16" (50.8 x 40.6 cm)
2-D layered paper collage
Artist's collection, Seattle

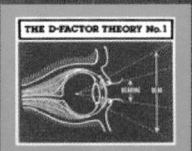
break, she noticed a commotion in the airport and walked away with the autograph of the Prime Minister of Vietnam, later learning she was also on the evening news. This woman stopped Meryl Streep on the street in New York and asked her to wait while she ran up to get her camera. Streep was still there when she returned. She introduced herself to Gene Wilder and Richard Pryor while they were filming a movie near her home and charmed her way into a press interview with them, ending by Mr. Wilder surprising her with a home-cooked lunch for the two of them in his set trailer. She found herself in Japan and within days of her arrival she was living with a Deaf host family and being interviewed on Japanese TV.

She has chutzpah, wit, and style in her five-foot frame. When I tell you she has been Deaf from birth, I expect some readers will be more impressed. As Silver would say, "Pfft. Get over yourself." Being Deaf is a part of her, like being born Jewish or being born a lesbian. It isn't amazing that she has done what she's done because she's Deaf. She is just amazing.

This book is an art biography because it is about her art, but it is also about her life. It reads in chronological format, starting with her birth and leads the reader through various stages in her life and artwork up to the present.

Ann vs. Silver

Silver is the preferred name for Ann Silver by Silver herself. I came to realize that few people have ever asked her what name she prefers. When I did so, I learned it wasn't Ann— she has never loved the name. She has signed most of her artwork *Silver* since 1966. For this reason, you will notice that the name Ann is not mentioned throughout the rest of the book, but Silver is used instead to refer to the artist known as Ann Silver. This book uses comments in blue as direct quotes from Silver over the last year of discussions with her. I freely admit I have noticed similarities between a few of the quotes and stories she has shared with me firsthand over many hours of meeting with her in person to direct quotes from various books and publications that have included her writing or have included excerpts of interviews of her. I assure

▲ SELF PORTRAIT | 1993
8" x 10" (20.3 x 25.4 cm)
ink on paper
Artist's collection, Seattle

you that she said these things to me, though she may have said them before. When I asked her about this, she told me that in some cases, she liked the way an idea was stated long before she was ever interviewed the first time, and she has answered some questions similarly her whole life.

Pop Art

While Silver has adopted a Japanese view of fame and is a relatively humble person, she considers herself a master of Deaf Pop Art. Before I can discuss what this is, a discussion of both Pop Art and Deaf Art seems prudent.

The first pieces now labeled as Pop Art were created in England in the late 1950s. Pop Art was a reaction against the big business of art as much as it was an attempt at blurring the lines between art and non-art. Of note, David Hockney, one of the early British Pop Artists, is deaf.

Pop Art is similar to *Dadaism,* a earlier movement that was started during the First World War as a negative reaction by artists against the atrocities of war. Dadaism positioned itself as an affront to logic, preferring intuition and nonsense.

Pop Art rebels against the art establishment's decree of what art *should* be. Pop Art uses common themes seen in everyday life by common people and makes art from them. During the 1960s many wondered if it was really art. Pop Art could be understood by regular people and it focused on items and ideas known to them.

At first, many Pop artists did not try to make their work clever. They didn't highly modify what they were depicting with deeper themes. They were trying to use humor to poke fun at art by selecting unusual subjects for high art. Andy Warhol (1928-1987) depicted cans of soup, soft drink bottles and multiple images of famous people. Roy Lichtenstein (1923-1997) enlarged comic strips, boxes of soap, mirrors, and living room layouts. David Hockney (b. 1937) painted the water in his pool and made portraits of ordinary people. Jasper Johns (b. 1930) painted targets and maps and U.S. flags. These were all relatively easy things to understand. As time went on, more complex ideas were expressed and some put deeper meaning into the work.

Deaf Art

The over-arching focus of Deaf Art is that its theme is about the Deaf experience. Limiting my discussion to the United States, there have been artists who are deaf since early colonial society, but they did not all produce what now is called Deaf Art. Although one can find and label earlier artists' work as Deaf Art, the Deaf Art Movement began on the campus of Gallaudet University in 1968. Although a 1989 Deaf Art manifesto (called

Silver signing DEAF ART, 1978

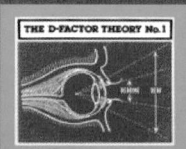

Silver permed, 1976

De'VIA) attempted to pigeonhole and set parameters for its expression, there is no specific formula for the medium, colors or style of visual art for the genre of Deaf Art. Body parts such as hands, arms, ears, eyes and faces are often used in many artists' work of this genre. An artist, however, who never depicts an ear or eye, is no less a part of the Deaf Art genre if their work speaks of the Deaf experience. Themes of oppression, cultural freedom, paternalism, cultural unity, American Sign Language, a celebration of community—all of these are an equal part of Deaf Art.

Chapter 5: DEAF ART MOVEMENT is dedicated to this aspect later in the book so please refer to this chapter for a greater understanding of the Deaf Art Movement.

Deaf Pop Art

Silver is not the only Deaf artist to use Pop Art themes in her work. She is, however, the first. Her first parody product, **SIGN EASY**, was produced in 1969 (in Chapter 3: BORN AGAIN DEAF). Her style has been imitated but she doesn't complain about that. After all, Silver imitates the work of others to some extent, but credit should be given where credit is due.

What is Deaf Pop Art? The playbook for this must start with a serious look at Silver's work. Like Warhol, she uses her graphic design background to create her work. Although her two-dimensional layered collage technique is dissimilar to Warholian screenprinting, it produces equally vibrant work. From her many years as a book illustrator, then book cover designer, then art director, she has a keen eye for precise and clean lines and it shows in her pieces.

Like other Pop artists, Silver takes common objects as the subject of many pieces of her work. Unlike early Pop Art, however, she parodies the products. She uses parody, but not just for a laugh. She makes a can of soup stand for her alma mater, and as a statement about the importance of Deaf culture (**GALLAUDET'S DEAF STUDIES SOUP GROUP** | 1992). She takes a bottle cap and points out the injustice of implanting the ears of babies (**Co-Chlear** | 1996). She takes a box of laundry soap and makes it a rallying point of Deaf community, (**DEAF PRIDE** | 1996). She takes a baby food jar and makes it an identifier of healthy language development for Deaf children (**SILVER BABY SIGNS** | 2012). She takes a periodic table and makes it into a classroom course on the Deaf World (**THE PERIODIC TABLE OF DEAF CULTURE** | 2012). She employs common road signs to say 100 things about culture, language, oppression and success. Examples can be found in Chapter 11: ROAD SIGNS.

Silver sets the bar high for the

Silver before heading to Japan, 1985

9: Mmm Mmm DEAF, Chapter 11: ROAD SIGNS, and Chapter 12: ARTISTIC ACTIVISM. Work from this period is also spread throughout the book. The book closes with more recent work found in Chapters 13 and 14.

Notes for the Reader

The artwork seen in each chapter is not entirely chronological. I often selected pieces that were inspired by experiences that happened during a period of time in her life, although the artwork itself may have been created at a different point in her life. Accurate dates of all artwork can be found in the labels near each piece in the book.

The labeling structure is:
Line 1: title, year
Line 2: width and height in
    inches and centimeters (cm)
Line 3: medium
Line 4: ownership and location

For artwork done by people other than Silver, this is noted between lines 1 and 2.

My apologies to the towns of Chicago, Wisconsin and Indianapolis, Oklahoma—iconic city names are used without state names. For example, Seattle for Seattle, WA; Chicago for Chicago, IL; and Indianapolis for Indianapolis, IN.

micro-genre of Deaf Pop Art. The formula for Deaf Pop Art might read one part common object, two parts parody, two parts wit, two parts deeply-relevant cultural theme, and three parts technical precision.

Chapter Synopsis

This book will cover Silver's upbringing and education in Chapters 2-4, then discuss her career as a graphic designer and illustrator of children's books and ASL dictionaries in both Washington DC and New York (Chapter 4: BORN AGAIN DEAF). It will touch on her work as a book cover designer working for several major publishers including Ballantine Books, Ace Books, Random House and Prentice-Hall. The book also includes Silver's work with her own company, Silversign, where she designed many greeting cards and logos for other companies and for her own use. Examples can be seen in Chapter 6: DEAF HEART NY.

Most of the book is focused on her artwork since 1991. After moving back to Seattle, Silver has had a lot to say in her art which can be found in Chapter

Chapter 2
SIGNS OF LIFE

Silver and her mother Belle, home from the hospital, 1949

SILVER WAS BORN INTO A HEARING family in Seattle, Washington in 1949. Her mother Belle had time to stay at home and attend to her daughter's every need. It was a time when a silent war was going on. This particular war was not the conflict that preceded the Korean War; it was what is known as the 100-Year War, or the Oral-Manual Debate. Silver was born when hip and famous people like Spencer Tracy were supporting the use of speech for teaching deaf children to the exclusion of Sign Language (the oralists). Her birthday, May 25, 1949, was sixteen long years before American Sign Language would be studied and named and she was never shown any signs as a baby.

Opening the chapter is an iconic product: a baby food jar. With its bright green, blue and yellow colors it portrays a non-food item that is nonetheless nutritious for the minds of children. Regardless of their hearing status, babies' brains are ready to process aspects of language before their vocal mechanisms are ready. Silver also cleverly uses her name to reflect a more iconic brand for baby food.

With hope that from now on all babies will be fed a complete diet of ASL, **SILVER BABY SIGNS** shows her strong support for the use of ASL in the lives of children in this colorful piece bearing her own likeness as an infant.

SILVER BABY SIGNS | 2012 ▲
16" x 20" (40.6 x 50.8 cm)
2-D digital collage
Private collection, California

Silver family photo, c. 1950

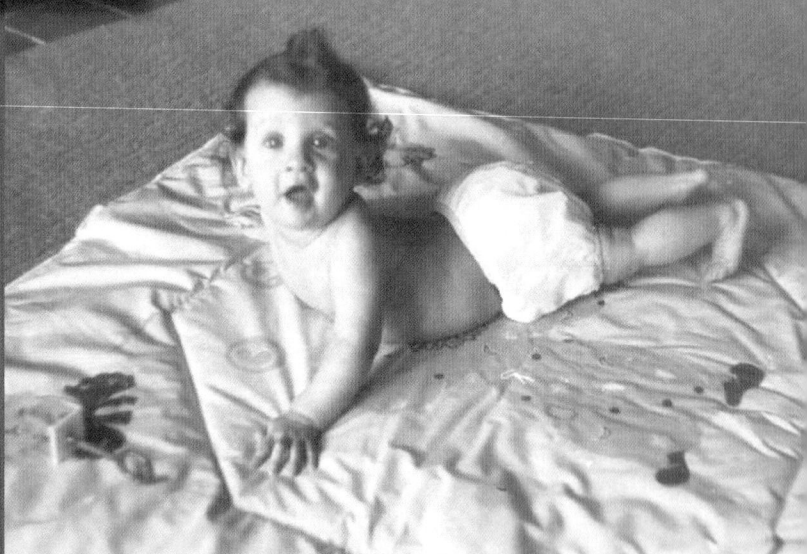

Silver handstand, c. 1950

Silver headstand, c. 1950

Silver on blanket c. 1950

Silver, Steve and Nancy, c. 1953

Silver's 5th birthday, 1954

TRULY EARLY WORK
(Untitled 1-4) | c. 1953
Pencil and crayons on paper
Artist's collection, Seattle

"I began art as soon as I entered the world (rumors of my scribbling on the walls inside my mother's womb cannot be confirmed). I was born genetically deaf into an all hearing family in Seattle. Art was my native language. I knew how to draw and communicate via art long before I ever learned English or American Sign Language (ASL). Does this make me trilingual?"

11

Ice Cream Communication

The Journey

to the

Ice Cream

On her way to get ice cream!
Silver, 1952

"I was the baby of three kids. When my brother and sister would be at school, or wherever they went when they weren't in front of me, I would poke my mother and show her a picture I had drawn. I drew using mostly pens and crayons. The first picture I drew was of her and I leaving our house. I pointed at Mom, then at the picture of her until she got the idea. Then I would point at another of us walking past a tree, then point at another of us walking past buildings. After several pictures, I pointed at one of me holding a big ice cream cone.

Mom had to read between the lines, or between the pictures. I really don't know how she did it. Looking back, she also had to read my mind! I never drew any buildings or trees, just pictures of us standing! Next I pointed at the refrigerator, she opened it and I pointed at the icebox. I was doing this to show her it was cold. I was playing charades. You want ICE CREAM? ICE CREAM?, she said it over and over. I craved ice cream. She got her purse and we walked to the store and she pointed at the freezer case and said, is that what you want? I nodded my head until it almost came off."

Store, c. 1953

1/5   Silver '92

GOOD DEAF HUMOR | 1992 ▲
20" x 16" (50.8 x 40.6 cm)
2-D layered paper collage
Private collection, Colorado

The bright blue circles against red vertical stripes reflect well in front of a large white square on a royal blue background. Centered on all this, jolly letters entice all who see it to enjoy GOOD DEAF HUMOR.

Deaf Roots

Although her parents were not deaf, Silver has several Deaf relatives on her mother's side. The Berchansky family arrived in Canada from Russia in 1905. There are two Deaf brothers and a sister depicted in this family photo.

Berchansky family photo, c. 1907
Green– Sam (Shimka) Berchansky (1894-1953)
Yellow– David Berchansky (1897-1956)
Red–Rebeka (Rivka) Berchansky (1877-?)

The Myth

"This story was told many times during my childhood at family gatherings. It always started with the time when my ancestors lived in the Ukraine. The Cossacks would come to the village of Dneprpetrovsk and harass and beat up the Jews who lived there. One time the Cossacks came through on their horses and **beat the ears** of some unfortunate family member. I assumed that meant smacking the poor guy or gal on both sides of the head. As the story goes, that was when the first person in the Berchansky family became deaf and it supposedly only impacts every other generation, at least that's the way I remember the story from my childhood growing up in Seattle as a young Silver family member."

—Steve Silver, brother

Rivka Berchansky
with two of her three children

Shimka and David Berchansky, c. 1911

Although younger, David was four inches taller than Shimka. They both attended the Manitoba School for the Deaf in Winnipeg at least for a short time around 1911. The two of them emigrated to the U.S. in 1919 and listed New York City as their final destination. Rivka, their Deaf sister who was much older than them, elected to stay behind in Winnipeg. She married and had three children. The two men found work as tailors in New York. Shimka never married, but David did and had two children. The men died during the 1950s and are buried in the Deaf section of the Beth-El cemetery in New Jersey.

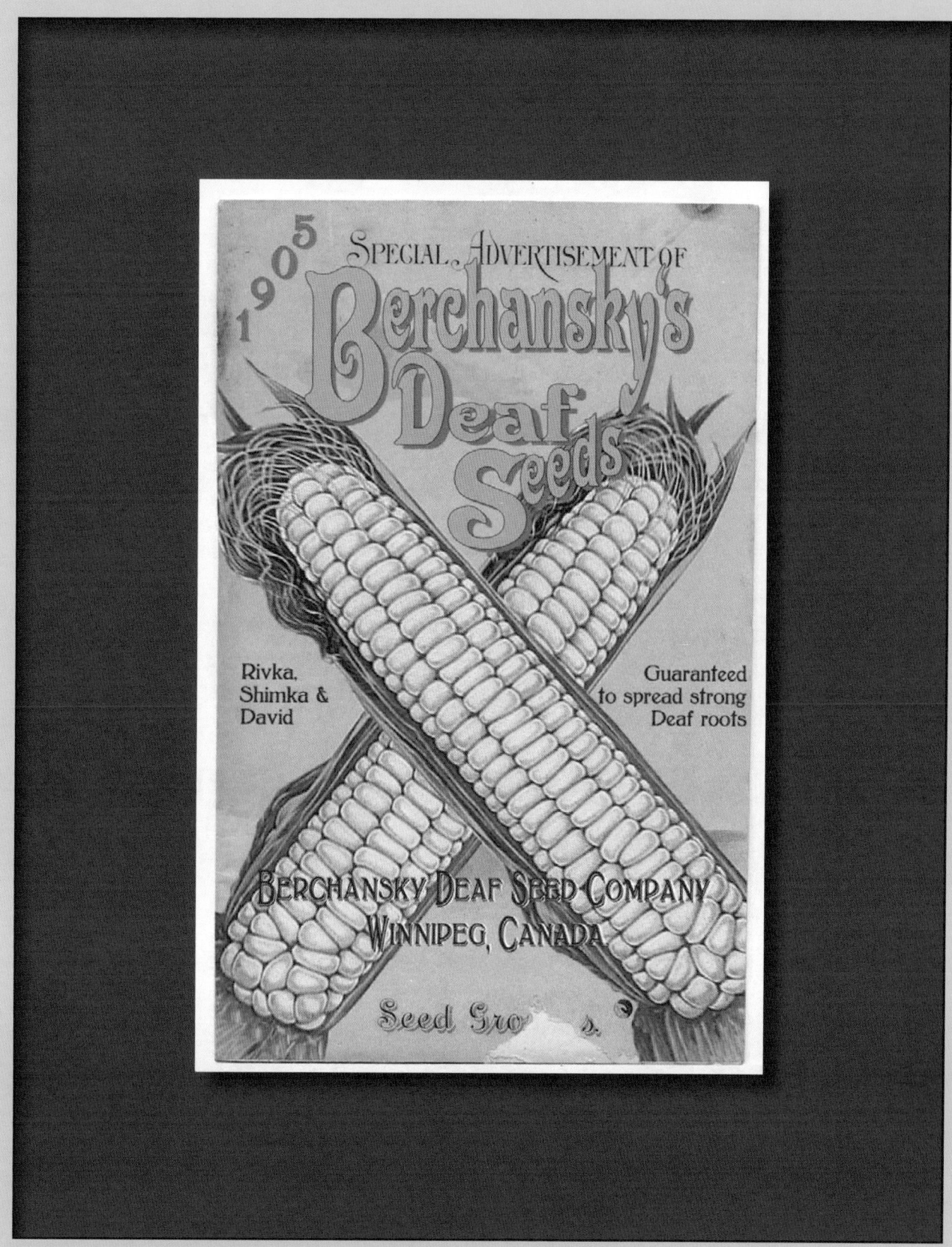

BERCHANSKY'S DEAF SEEDS | 2012 ▲
4" x 6" (10.2 x 15.2 cm)
Digital neo-vintage seed package by **SILVER MOON** BRAND
Artist's collection, Seattle

SIGNS OF LIFE

"Hearing" Deaf and Dumb

"In a 5th grade math class, I saw the score of boy behind me and blurted out that I had, once again, gotten a higher mark. He gave me a sour look and blurted out something of his own. I didn't know what Deaf and Dumb was, but I knew he wasn't supposed to call me that. I raised my hand and repeated what he called me to the teacher and saw him get scolded for it. I went home and asked the question parents of Deaf kids must dread-- 'Mommy, what does Deaf and Dumb mean?' I learned later that my brother and sister would frequently stand up for me, telling their friends not to call me that. I must have been called that 50 times or more before that day in 5th grade when my mother sat me in her lap and explained. My god."

Taxi! Taxi!

Silver takes a taxi to school, c. 1955

Silver often took a taxi because it was a benefit given to the deaf students of her school. Her mother was thrilled when they were assigned a rare female cab driver with whom Silver and Belle bonded a bit over the years.

Silver dons a mono-hearing aid, c. 1957

Mrs. Taxi and Silver pose, c. 1955

"I hated wearing hearing aids. In fact, I threw mine out of the rolled-down window on more than one occasion without the cabbie's knowledge."

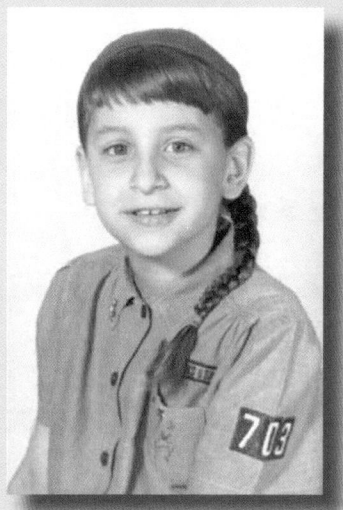

As a Brownie, c. 1957

1956

Class photo (Silver on far right), 1956

The Encyclopedia

"One Sunday afternoon when I was about ten, I was browsing through our new complete set of the Encyclopedia Britannica that my parents had purchased by installments. Picking out the 'D' volume at random, I turned page by page with great interest until I came to the word 'deaf.' My mind froze in alarm. I remembered the label 'deaf' was applied to me. I was never really conscious or fully aware of being deaf-as-different in my life up to that time. The article was a dawning of understanding for me. The more I re-read the section, the more confused I became about myself. The article had emphasized that being deaf causes various problems and difficulties. The statement gave me true concern.

My mother came in the room just at that time, admiring what I was doing. I had a mean and unpleasant look on my face and I exploded at her, 'why did you make me deaf?' Mother was thrown off guard, but she patiently explained in detail about me being genetically deaf and how it was not intentional. She did say that being deaf had its share of problems.

There was a long silence.

During the quiet, my anxieties and fears vanished. I cocked my head and said with a sly grin, 'Mom, that's all right. Being deaf isn't a problem for me. But about my brother... HE is a problem for me!'"

George (father) and Silver, c. 1959

A Glimpse of ASL

"Although now it is a faint memory, I recall that I was watching TV and my mother went to open the front door. She came back to me and motioned for me and asked me to follow her. I did so and I saw a middle-aged man at the door. I had never seen him before.

Mom said, 'He is deaf like you.' I didn't understand. I didn't have a Deaf identity at that time. He was the first deaf adult I had seen in my life. I think I was 9 years old. Although I was unaware of it at the time, I see now that it was my first exposure to ASL. He tried to sign to me. I was not allowed to do that and I only understood his final gesture. He held out his hand asking me if I wanted his card. It was a card containing a miniature version of the ASL fingerspelled alphabet, slightly larger than a business card.

I had no concept of what it meant to be a peddler, I just looked at him with wide eyes, not taking the card. Mom took over and politely told him no. I didn't understand what was going on when she closed the door. Looking back, I don't think my mother would have supported any person going door to door asking for cash, regardless of his or her hearing status.

Within 30 minutes of her shutting the door, my mother got several phone calls from neighbors stating that there was a deaf man at their door— several asked if we knew him or if perhaps I should meet him. They thought I could somehow benefit by talking with him. Because he used Sign Language and I was not allowed to do that, I think she was trying to tell them it was a bad idea. I suppose she corrected them, telling them that she believed that I would need to speak English aloud and know how to lipread to be successful as a deaf person.

I certainly had a lot of spies in my neighborhood…"

Silver's braided triptych, c. 1958

This piece represents a twist on the typical ABC card that a peddler might have passed to potential givers. The brown background hosts a bright orange card depicting the ASL fingerspelled alphabet of the late 1800's. A miniature lantern is attached to show the importance of light to seeing ASL. The lime green card shows mouth movements and points out the difficulty of lipreading. As a humorous corollary, a box of "Oral Mints for nasty breath" is attached to the oral peddler card.

PEDDLER CULTURE 101 | 1996 ▶
16" x 20" (40.6 x 50.8 cm)
2-D layered paper collage with attached trinkets
Private collection, Pennsylvania

PEDDLER CULTURE 101

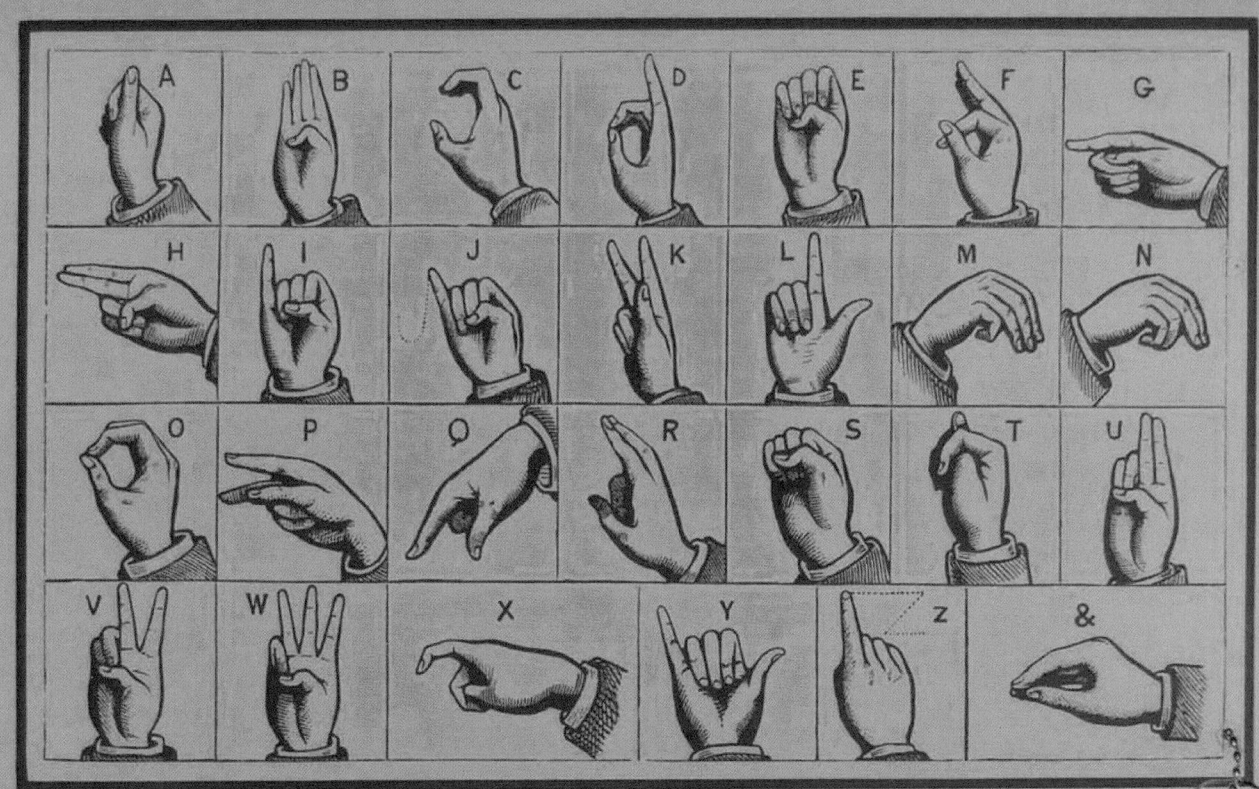

Chapter 3
ART 101

SAILBOAT | 1967 ▼
15.75" x 12" (40 x 30.5 cm)
watercolor on paper
Artist's collection, Seattle

"AS A CLASSIC BY-PRODUCT OF SO-CALLED deaf education, I was schooled the hard way. ASL interpreters and note taking services were non-existent in my time. Though I don't blame my parents, as common sense in this area was trained out of them, I was strictly forbidden to use ASL. I did not do so until I was on my own in college. As the only Deaf student in my high school class, my educational method was 50% book reading and 50% pure guesswork. Although I was required to sit in front of all my classes, the goal of this was rarely met. It was impossible to lipread through the back of the teacher's head when he or she wrote on the blackboard, and impossible for me to turn fast enough to lipread students who were behind me. No one should be educated that way.

I was raised believing that when I finished high school I would, 'lead a normal life as a hearing person.' This led me to believe my hearing ability would be restored! I was not exposed to one Deaf role model or leader until after I graduated from high school and was on my own."

▲ READ MY LIPS / READ MY MIND | 1992
20" x 16" (50.8 x 40.6 cm)
2-D layered paper collage
Artist's collection, Seattle

THREE BOTTLES STILL LIFE | 1967 ▲
15.75" x 12" (40 x 30.5 cm)
watercolor on paper
Artist's collection, Seattle

▲ **HOLY TOLEDO** | 1966
60" x 48" (152.4 x 121.9 cm)
paint & marker on paper
Artist's collection, Seattle

SEVEN APPLES STILL LIFE | 1967 ▲
15.75" x 12" (40 x 30.5 cm)
watercolor on paper
Artist's collection, Seattle

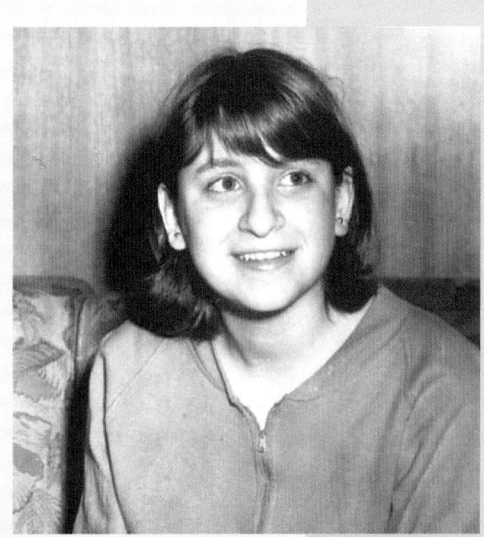

Silver in high school, c. 1967

▲ LAKE LANDSCAPE | 1967
15.75" x 12" (40 x 30.5 cm)
watercolor on paper
Artist's collection, Seattle

▲ MUGS STILL LIFE | 1967
15.75" x 12" (40 x 30.5 cm)
watercolor on paper
Artist's collection, Seattle

▲ ABSTRACT | 1967
12" x 15.75" (30.5 x 40 cm)
watercolor on paper
Artist's collection, Seattle

▲ FISH & EGGS STILL LIFE | 1967
11" x 17.5" (27.9 x 44.4 cm)
watercolor on paper
Artist's collection, Seattle

14   Roosevelt High School, Seattle, Wash. 98115

Ann Silver To Do Sketches, Cartoons For RHS News

That's what's holding up our report cards...

Ann Silver, senior, will draw political and school activity cartoons for future editions of the **Roosevelt News.**

Ann designed the activity card this year, the basketball program covers for every home game, various signs for school activities, and has sketched for La Douce Vie and Lab Writer, Roosevelt literary publications.

During Seafair, Ann sketched scenes from the hydroplane races and sold them.

The senior got first place in the State final in the American Legion Poppy Poster Contest two years ago. Last year she was one of ten first place winners in the U.S. Hearing-Aid

Manufacturer's Corp. Christmas Card Designs Contest.

Ann's mother first discovered Ann had artistic talent. "At the age of three, I climbed upon the bar in the recreation room and drew pictures on the ceiling!" Ann related.

"So one day I pick up a pencil and scribble, and the scribble is pleasing to my conscious and subconscious mind, so I continue. I love the feeling that comes when a painting starts to click. I crave it," she continued.

Ann, who is Girls' Club Corresponding Secretary and a Spur, has considered teaching for the deaf at the high school level.

"That's what's holding up our report cards..."
Roosevelt High School newspaper article, 1967

▲ HOT - KOSHER - COLD | 1966
8.5" x 11" (21.6 x 27.9 cm)
Pen and pencil on paper
Artist's collection, Seattle

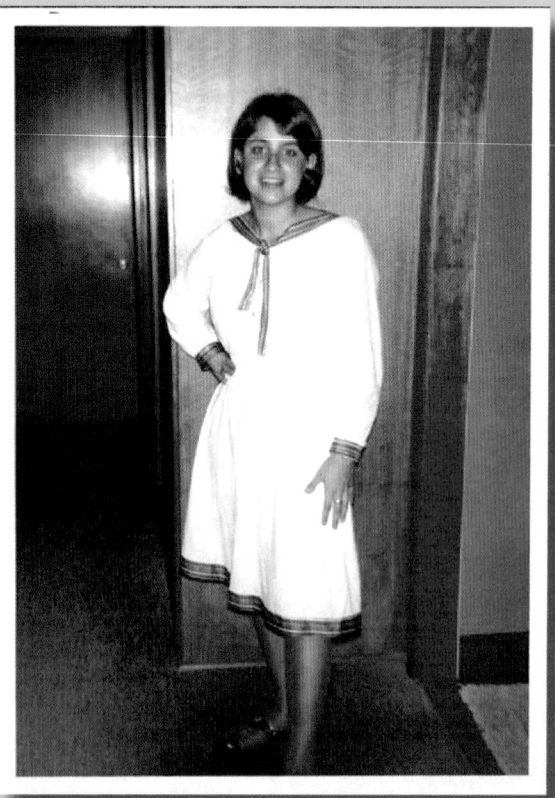

Silver at home, 1968

QUARTERBACKING | 1966 ▶
18" x 24" (45.7 x 60.9 cm)
Watercolor on paper
Artist's collection, Seattle

▲ **PEACE** | 1966
8.5" x 11" (21.6 x 27.9 cm)
Pen and pencil on paper
Artist's collection, Seattle

◀ **IS SHE OR
ISN'T SHE?** | 1966
24" x 18" (60.9 x 45.7 cm)
Watercolor on paper
Artist's collection, Seattle

Robert E. (Ned) Behnke

Ned Behnke (1948-1989) was one of Silver's childhood friends who lived in Seattle and was also Deaf. He introduced Silver to gourmet dining, skiing, subtitled foreign films and many other things. Though they attended different high schools, their mutual love of art kept them in touch with each other and they attended many social events together.

Ned and Silver last saw each other in 1968. He attended Central Washington State University and then attended the National Technical Institute for the Deaf (NTID) at the Rochester Institute of Technology, where he was certainly exposed to ASL, and earned his MFA in painting.

Ned was an excellent artist and has the distinction of being the first Deaf artist to win a fine arts award from Rochester's Memorial Art Gallery and had the honor of a solo show there one year later. His work is in the permanent collections of prominent institutions in the Seattle area.

Ned is memorialized by the *Neddy at Cornish*, an annual awards program sponsored by the Behnke Foundation that celebrates his passion and life as an artist by giving the Neddy Awards, two unrestricted financial awards to artists living and working in the Puget Sound area.

Ned Behnke, 1967

"*Around 1963, Ned and I saw a watercolor painting at the Hearing, Speech & Deaf Center. The artwork by Morris Broderson depicted fingerspelling. Ned and I were shocked. We would never have considered this acceptable behavior for an artist. We were taught not to use signs and here they were immortalized in a painting! It gave us a lot to consider and was our first exposure to what later came to be known as Deaf Art.*"

▲ MERGE / NO MAINSTREAMING | 1992
20" x 16" (50.8 x 40.6 cm)
2-D layered paper collage
Private collection, Rhode Island

Depicting a single sign containing two pieces of information, this is one of only two road signs Silver made of this type. The iconic circle-slash *DO NOT* symbol stands out boldly in red against the black-lettered white sign.

Mainstreaming is a term that has been replaced with the term inclusion, but both mean the same thing— placing Deaf children in schools with hearing children. For many of these children, such placement is not the least restrictive environment if communication access is not present. When Silver was mainstreamed, she felt like the classroom's Deaf mascot. She was never provided an interpreter or notetaker. In this piece, she says the thoughtless practice of placing children in schools using interpreters instead of having teachers who are trained to teach students directly should be discouraged, if not banned completely.

ART 101

◀ FOREST | 1967
15.75" x 12" (40 x 30.5 cm)
watercolor on paper
Artist's collection, Seattle

▼ GIRLS' CLUB AGENDA | 1967
8.5" x 11" (21.6 x 27.9 cm)
mimeograph
Artist's collection, Seattle

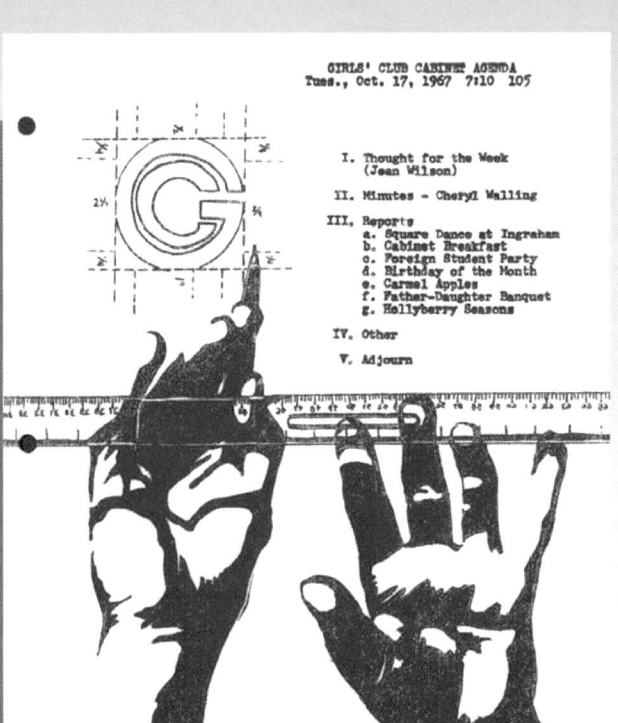

Silver and Ned Behnke, 1967

▲ SHORELINE VS. ROOSEVELT | 1967
11" x 8.5" (27.9 x 21.6 cm)
mimeograph
Artist's collection, Seattle

Silver created these programs for high school basketball games which were sold as a fundraiser for 10 cents each. Notice the detail on the Official Basketball Signals.

◀ ROOSEVELT VS. BALLARD | 1967
5.5" x 8.5" (14 x 21.6 cm)
mimeograph
Artist's collection, Seattle

Chapter 4

BORN AGAIN DEAF

SILVER'S YEARS AT GALLAUDET IN Washington DC occurred before the advent of closed-captioned TV, before TTYs, and before text relay services. It was long before the Americans with Disabilities Act (ADA) was passed and long before the Deaf President Now movement. Awareness of American Sign Language was in its nescient stage and awareness of Deaf culture was far from a reality.

Silver graduation photo, 1972

Silver was in the nation's Capitol at a time when the civil rights movement was making headlines, but disability rights and Deaf rights were not yet a reality. She was one of the few people who pointed out the inequity and has been doing so all her life.

On a brown gradient background this white sign with bright blue and white lettering opens the chapter standing as a warning. There are some places where languages cross each other's paths. The shadow on the post and the realistic overlaid screws have made observers wonder if it is a photograph of a real sign.

For Silver, this linguistic crossing was quite real for her when she arrived at Gallaudet College (now Gallaudet University).

ASL & ENGLISH LINGUISTIC X-ING | 1992 ▲
16" x 20" (40.6 x 50.8 cm)
2-D digital collage
Private collection, California

Chapter 4

BORN AGAIN DEAF

▲ HARRY R. WILLIAMS | 1969
13.5" x 18" (34.3 x 45.7 cm)
ink on paper
Artist's collection, Seattle

Harry R. Williams

Silver and HRW took an instant liking to each other even before they took art clases together. When she arrived at Gallaudet she did not know ASL. Harry was from a Deaf family and signed fluently and beautifully.

Eventually the two of them worked out a deal. HRW helped improve Silver's ASL and she corrected his written English. They both struggled with the language they were learning yet they shared the language of art.

By the time Silver was a Junior, HRW declared her BAD—Born Again Deaf. This meant that she had a conversion experience and had come to accept her identity as a Deaf person.

"The artwork of Harry R. Williams (HRW) opened many eyes, mine included, to the visionary qualities of art from a Deaf perspective.

Every day with HRW was an intensive session in Deaf history and Deaf culture. He knew so much about Deaf artists and their background! This was before there were any books about Deaf culture and before any knowledge of Deaf art. This guy had a great knack for remembering stories he had been told and for putting together different clues to make his understanding of an artist's background complete."

▲ HRW | 1969
17" x 28" (43.1 x 71.1 cm)
marker on paper
Artist's collection, Seattle

David Peikoff

David Peikoff is a distant relative of Silver's equal to the younger cousin of her grandfather. He attended the same school for the Deaf at the same time as her own grand-uncles in the early 1900s.

Peikoff became well known for his alumni work at Gallaudet, raising hundreds of thousands of dollars for the restoration of Ole' Jim, a beloved building on campus that was renamed Peikoff Alumni House.

Silver's grandmother wrote to her cousin, David's sister, asking her to give her assurance that he would take care of Silver when she arrived on campus. David sent a letter in May, before Silver graduated from high school, assuring his sister and Silver's grandmother that he would "*do what needed to be done*" to assure that Silver was taken care of while at Gallaudet.

With careful words, he assured his sister on his new Director of Development letterhead that Silver would be in the right place: "*No other campus offers as much in the all-around development of the deaf person. To be an expert lipreader is a fine accomplishment, but it is not everything. There must be more than that gift to be a success. It would be superfluous for me to go into all details on this complex subject but Ann will learn this to her advantage.*" He was telling her family that she would benefit from learning ASL at Gallaudet, but he knew better than to say it clearly to people who wouldn't understand the importance of ASL in the life of a Deaf person. His support for her in this way is incalculable to her life's success.

David Peikoff and Silver, 1972

"*When I visited Gallaudet in July of 1968, David Peikoff was our host and was very friendly showing us everything. We were given the royal treatment and he made us feel welcome.*

When I got to campus I saw him once the first week, and he told me he wouldn't be checking in on me frequently in person, but that I could call on him for anything I needed. I never called him, and therefore I barely saw him the four years I was at Gallaudet.

Years later I found out he gave his sister and my grandmother two or three glowing reports a year about my progress. Regardless of what trouble I might have been into, it was all positive. He was watching out for me without talking to me!"

A Debt of Thanks

Mildred M. Johnson

"In my life there have been people who have supported me and had vision for my life when I did not. I am indebted to a CODA (a person with Deaf parents) named Mildred M. Johnson who worked at the Division of Vocational Rehabilitation in Seattle. I had planned to attend college at Stanford University, although I had no idea how I was going to pay for it. Mildred strongly suggested that I attend Gallaudet College (now University) instead– and made it clear that if I were to do so, VR would pay my tuition, room and board there for four years. Her offer changed my life and ensured that I earned a college degree."

▲ CEREAL STUDY | 1969
8.5" x 11" (21.6 x 27.9 cm)
Ink on paper
Artist's collection, Seattle

With its bright yellow and black stripes, **CLIFFFS NOTETAKERS:** *Deaf Culture* is a parody of the crib-note book series that allows people to read a short version of a famous book or play. At the time Silver was in college, there were no textbooks on Deaf culture and there was no shortcut way to get a crash course in Deaf culture. One had to learn it from other Deaf people directly.

Note the optical illusion in this piece. The diagonal lines makes it look as if it is not square on the page.

CLIFFFS NOTETAKERS: Deaf Culture | 1999 ▶
16" x 20" (40.6 x 50.8 cm)
2-D layered paper collage
Artist's collection, Seattle

DEAF
CULTURE

Cliffs®
NOTETAKERS INC.
YOUR KEY TO THE DEAF-WORLD

1/5   Silver '99

BORN AGAIN DEAF

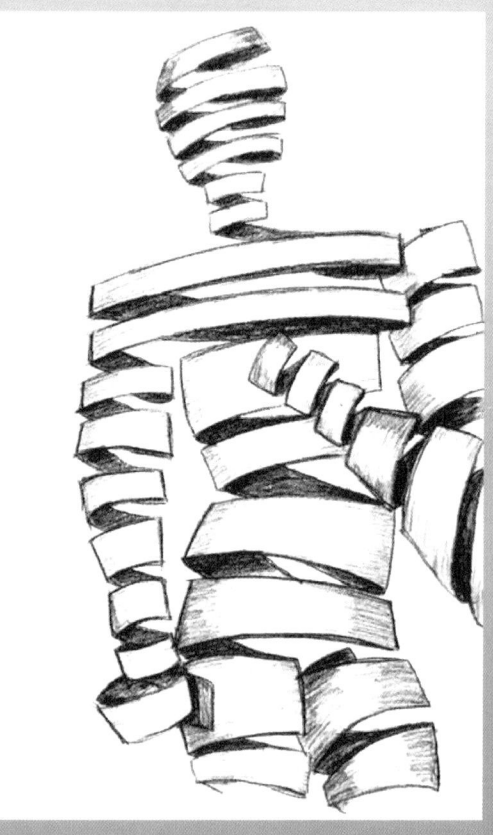

▲ PAPER RIBBON MAN | 1969
12" x 18" (30.5 x 45.7 cm)
graphite on paper
Artist's collection, Seattle

JACK FENNELL | 1969 ▲
17" x 21" (43.1 x 53.3 cm)
marker on paper
Artist's collection, Seattle

Photo by Chun Louie. Used with permission.

Silver "triplets," 1968

TWO MEN ON A BENCH | 1970 ▶
36" x 36" (91.4 x 91.4 cm)
Acrylic on canvas
Artist's collection, Seattle

Silver in front of her artwork, 1971

MOTORCYCLE | 1971 ▼
36" x 48" (91.4 x 121.6 cm)
Acrylic on canvas
Artist's collection, Seattle

Silver irreverently half sits on the lap of the Gallaudet and Alice statue for her graduation photo from Gallaudet, 1972

37

BORN AGAIN DEAF

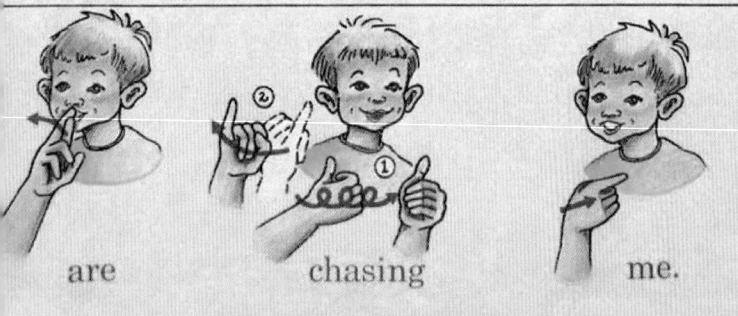

▲ ENHANCED PAGE 16 | 1974
(From Sand, Sea, Shells and Sky, 1974)
8" x 10" (20.3 x 25.4 cm)
ink over printed page
Artist's collection, Seattle

Signed English Books

Shortly before her graduation in 1972, Silver was approached by Dr. Harry Bornstein, the lead in creating a series of books using an invented signing system called *Signed English*.

Dr. Bornstein asked her if she wanted a job working with his team in illustrating books for children. She accepted the job and illustrated over 10 children's books and dictionaries over the next three years.

The Signed English system uses ASL signs with invented signs for endings of words like 'ing', 'ly', and 'ment'. They thought this system would make English easier for Deaf children to understand, but there has been no research that substantiates this.

Silver was not happy about including the Signed English artwork in this book. She wanted to be clear that she does not support the use of Signed English, but it is a part of her past. There are many others out there who may have supported it in the 1970s who no longer do so.

Her work was credited in these books, but her style and choices prove her work as much as her name. Notice the type of waves Silver chose for this illustration of a father and son playing in the ocean. They are waves reminiscent of Japanese painters like Katsushika Hokusai (1760-1849) who did Ukiyo-e painting during the Edo period. Who but Silver would have chosen this?

Silver at work, 1974

Finished illustration, 1973

Reference photo with graffiti à la Marcel Duchamp (for drawing angles that can't be seen by a mirror), 1973

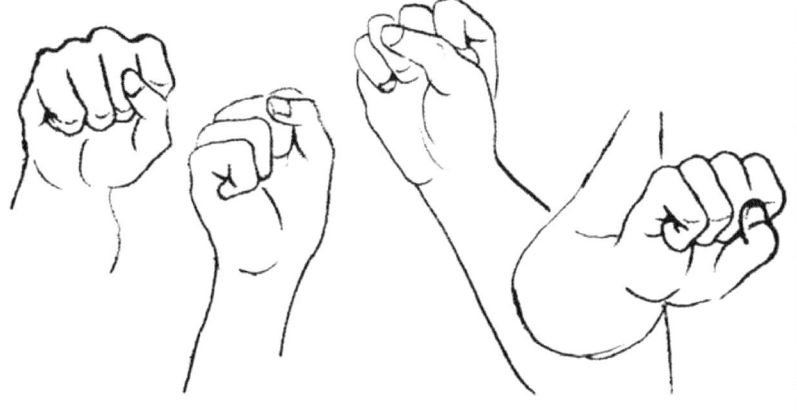
Reference drawings of fingerspelled S, 1973

Rough drawing and finished page for **The Three Billy Goats Gruff**, 1974

"I worked at Gallaudet for three years before a cataclysmic event ended my career there. A community firestorm erupted over Signed English. They called it one of the many artificial and oppressive signing systems invented by hearing people in the name of Deaf education.

This woke me up to negative power, communication abuse, and the bastardization of ASL. I felt I had to resign and embark on a lifelong journey of activism for Deaf rights.

So, in 1975 I loaded up a rental truck in the nations's capitol and headed for NYC with my friend Liz Baird to keep me company."

Chapter 5
DEAF ART MOVEMENT

SILVER ARRIVED ON GALLAUDET'S CAMPUS in fall 1968 and immediately started spending time in the Washburn Art Center where other art majors hung out. Harry R. Williams (HRW) was as much a leader of the group as anyone. Others that were involved at the time make an interesting list: Silver, HRW, John Darcy Smith, and John Canady were the core of many who would come and go. As time went on, this core group would paint as much for each other as for class assignments. They did portraits of each other both nude and clothed and kept pushing their own artistic understanding and limits.

This was the late 1960s and early 1970s in Washington DC. There was so much going on that would change our understanding of civil rights and the rights of women.

This piece is based on Silver's 1989 illustration made on a letter faxed to Betty G. Miller and Paul Johnston, co-organizers of the De'VIA workshop at the Deaf Way I Conference.

▲ DAM! (DEAF ART MOVEMENT), No. 2 | 2012
SILVER MOON BRAND
8.5" x 11" (21.6 x 27.9 cm)
Digital print on paper
Artist's collection, Seattle

DEAF ART MOVEMENT

There were many setbacks and leaps forward, but not at Gallaudet itself. A few steps outside the front gates changes could happen, but not inside.

The Chair of the Art Department was unmoved by students' frequent impassioned statements about their desire for more and innovative experiences.

Silver and HRW wanted to show the world something of what being Deaf was about. Hearing or Deaf– they just wanted to express their perspective.

It had only been three years since ASL was named by Silver's English teacher her freshman year. Dr. William C. Stokoe Jr. published *A Dictionary of American Sign Language on Linguistic Principles* in 1965. While the book is a landmark event in Deaf history, it took several years for this new label to stick. The book read like Chinese to

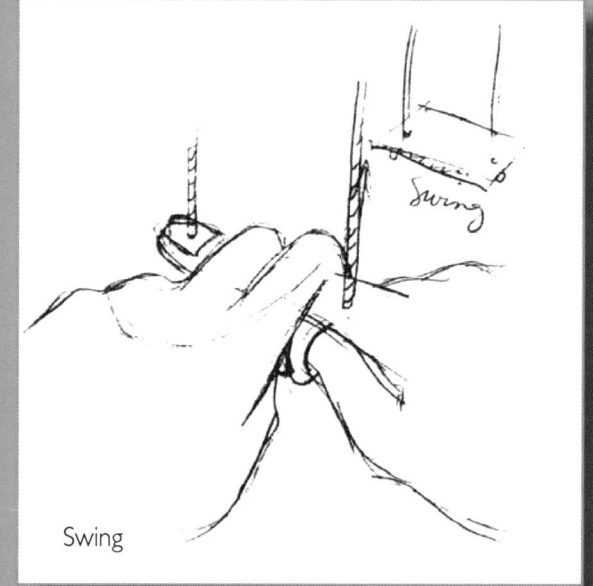

SWING: excerpt from proposal, 1971

most people. Deaf people often just called it the sign language. While there had been excellent presidents of the National Association of the Deaf since it was established in 1880, it wasn't until Silver's generation that people were taking a hard look at issues of access and rights of all disabled people. Don't forget that Silver was raised to believe she could make change happen. Her mother more than any other person showed her how this works and how being silent only means being passed over.

With Silver as the firecracker agitator riling up HRW and the boys, they tried in a variety of ways to make change at Gallaudet and succeeded in some unexpected ways.

In fall of 1971, Silver was a senior and had an idea. She suggested an independent study project to her primary art teacher, Betty G. Miller. She proposed creating a book full of signed art. She wanted to show objects

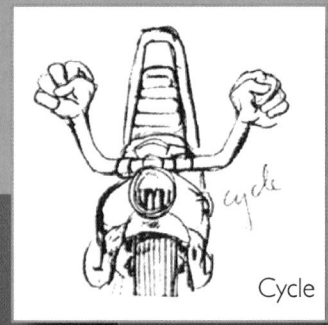

Cycle

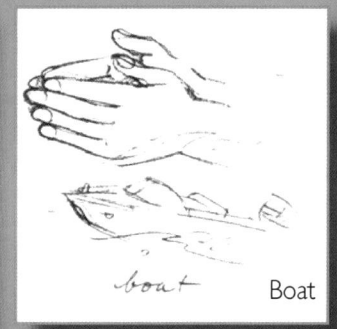

Boat

Plane

Binoculars

CYCLE, BOAT, PLANE and BINOCULARS: excerpt from proposal, 1971

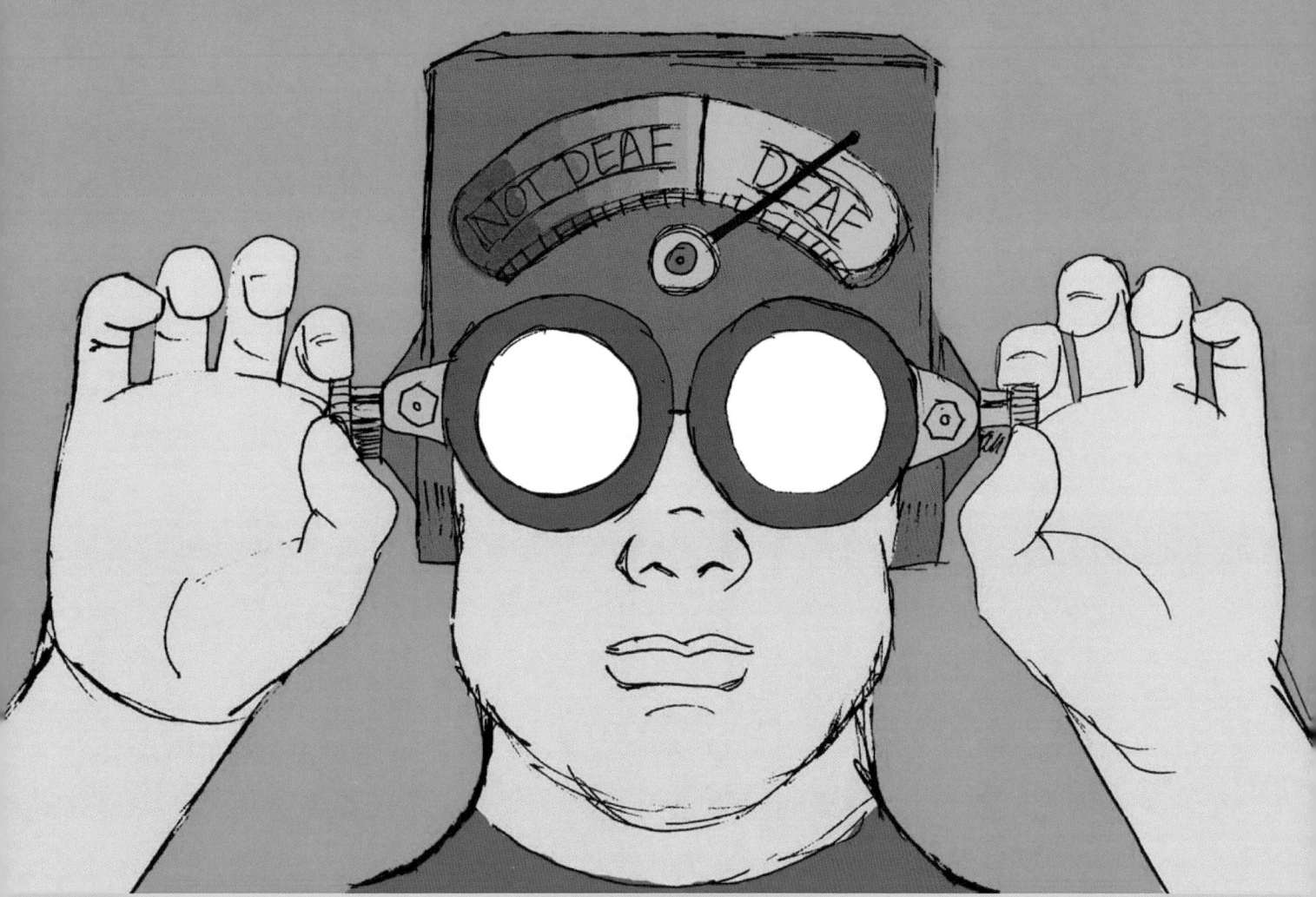

▲ DEAF-O-METER | 1969
11" x 8.5" (27.9 x 21.6 cm)
Ink on paper
(digitally colorized, 2012)
Artist's collection, Seattle

and ideas in the context of ASL. Silver wanted to have a sign depicting a helicopter that looked like a helicopter taking off using a hand as the propeller and another as its base. She intended to incorporate an artistic vision that was unheard of at that time and never before seen.

She had taken a couple of weeks over the summer to make sketches for a variety of signs that would work well for her book project and she was excited to show her professor her plan.

While it is not the desire of this author to remark poorly on Betty G. Miller, I must say that her decision to not support Silver's project was unfortunate. This was Deaf Art. This was an incorporation of language and art and wit. This was what every professor should dream for his or her students. To see a student reach for something grand and to be a part of such innovation is a privilege that none should pass up lightly.

As it happened, Miller had her reasons for making this decision. As Silver tells it, Miller did not react positively to her ideas and told her to not attempt to create art of this kind. She told Silver that it was not artistically worthy as a subject for students and suggested she work on something else.

Perhaps as a bone, Miller asked Silver to design a postcard announcing

her own upcoming art exhibit which was so top secret that she had not shown any of it to her students or fellow faculty.

Unwittingly, Silver agreed to support her teacher and created the postcard for the exhibit scheduled to open in February 1972. Between that fall and February, the Deaf Art Movement didn't sit back and wait for graduation. They instead started making a variety of 8mm films that lambasted the Art Department at Gallaudet. These films were art in their own right. They attempted to demonstrate the beauty of ASL and convince the faculty of the merit of using sign language in art.

Betty G. Miller asked the group if she could review the films and took them. The films were never rightfully returned.

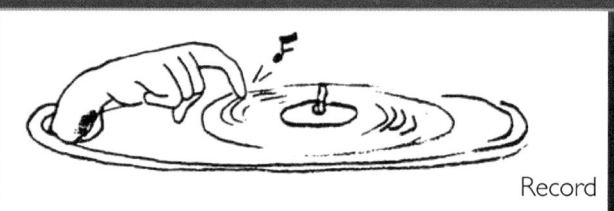

RECORD: excerpt from proposal, 1971

The Big Show

On Sunday, February 6, 1972, Betty G. Miller held an art exhibit that for the Deaf community at that time was a wondrous explosion of negative heat. In artistic terms, it was very Dadaist, a negative reaction to the oppression

(continued on page 48)

First Product

This image of a hand holding an small aerosol can on a teal background is the first product Silver ever created and may well be the oldest example of Deaf Pop Art.

Silver created this parody of a breath mint spray as a poignant reminder of her own desire for an instant way to improve her ASL skills. The handshape of the hand is also the same as a question mark in ASL, making one wonder if there is an implied question in this piece. Is it asking, *"Do you think learning ASL is easy?"*

Helicopter

HELICOPTER: excerpt from proposal, 1971

SIGN EASY | 1969 ▶
8.5" x 11" (21.6 x 27.9 cm)
Ink and marker on paper
(digitally colorized, 2012)
Artist's collection, Seattle

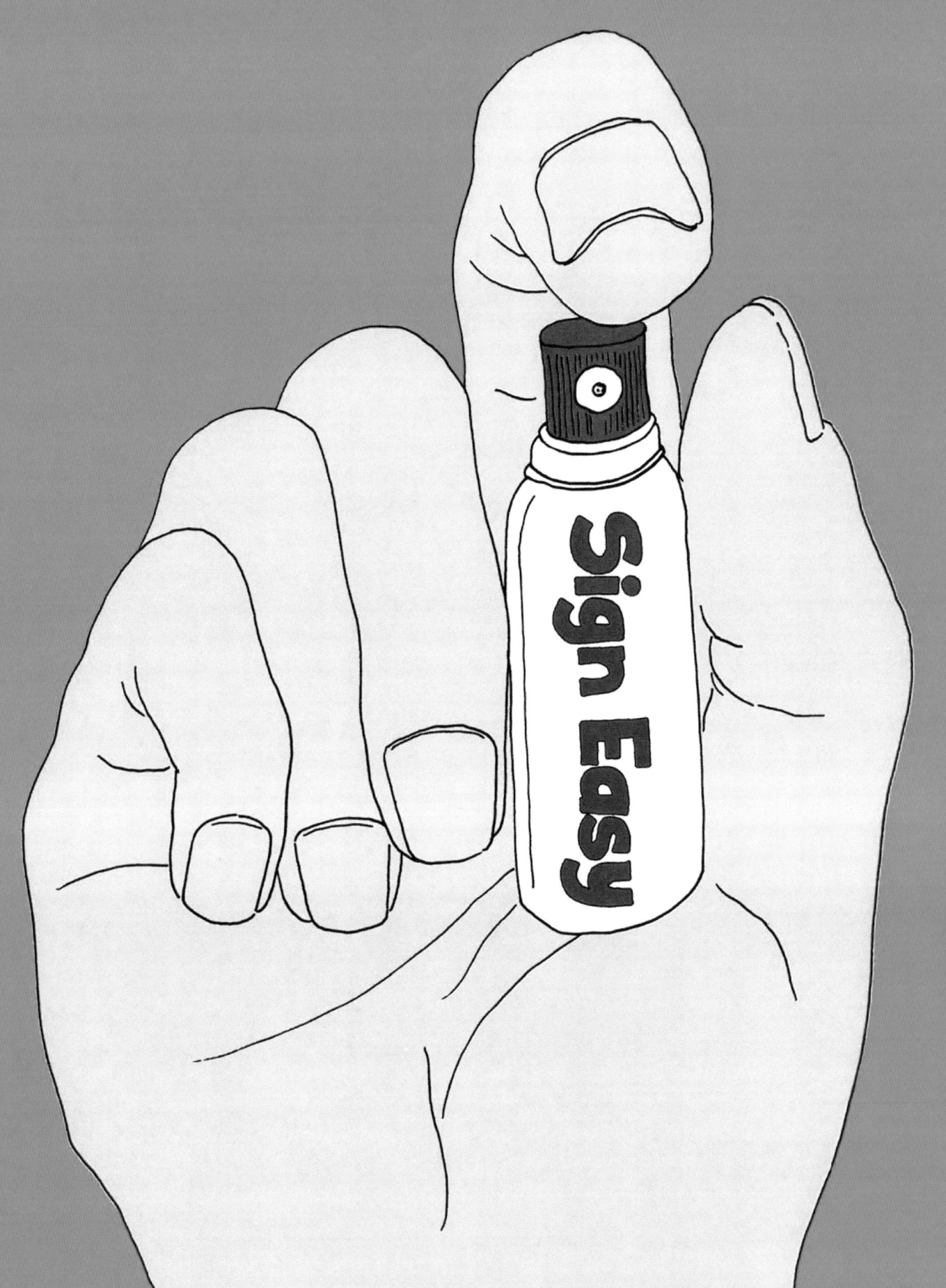

In Their Own Words

Silver was able to unearth a poor quality copy of one of the 8mm films that she made in 1971 of her and Harry R. Williams. Here is what they had to say in their own words:

"My Art proposal was totally rejected.

Hammer

Phone

HAMMER and PHONE
excerpt from proposal, 1971

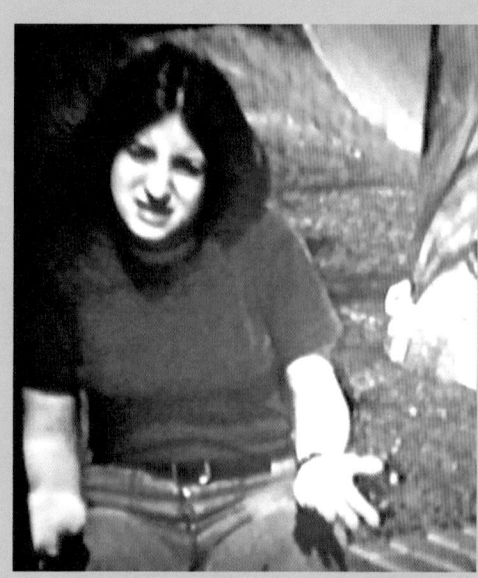

Come on,   why?"

"When I came to Gallaudet, I was so excited! I got to work on my art.

Then the Art Chair comes and cuts me off.

I said, 'Hey, I want to do more, study more.'

And I was told, 'Well, that's all there is for you.'

What a bummer."

— HRW

faced by children educated using only speech and lipreading. Silver and Miller both had this in their background. Miller, however, had parents who used ASL at home, perhaps making the concept of attempting education via speech and lipreading more difficult when one knows there is an easier more productive way used daily at home. Silver didn't have that balance. For her it was the same at school as it was at home.

Miller's show was a revelation and a landmark event. It is truly a shame that she couldn't have included the bright students looking for a champion for their cause of Deaf Art. Although she did have a show before these students could possibly have done so, there is no question that HRW, Silver, and other students who were part of the DAM were still looking for their chance to express their more positive ideas about Deaf Art, before, during, and after Miller's controversial show.

We are all a product of our time and in that time Gallaudet did not seem entirely hospitable to the needs of students. This was 16 years before a Deaf person would be president of Gallaudet University. The concept of crab theory or any social theory related to Deaf culture was years from being discussed, however it seems crab theory was at work here.

When crab fishermen catch crab they merely put them in an open bucket on top of each other. The crabs could climb out of the bucket, but whenever one gets close to the edge and is about to get out, another will immediately attempt to pull them back into the bucket, as if to say, "I can't get out, so you can't either."

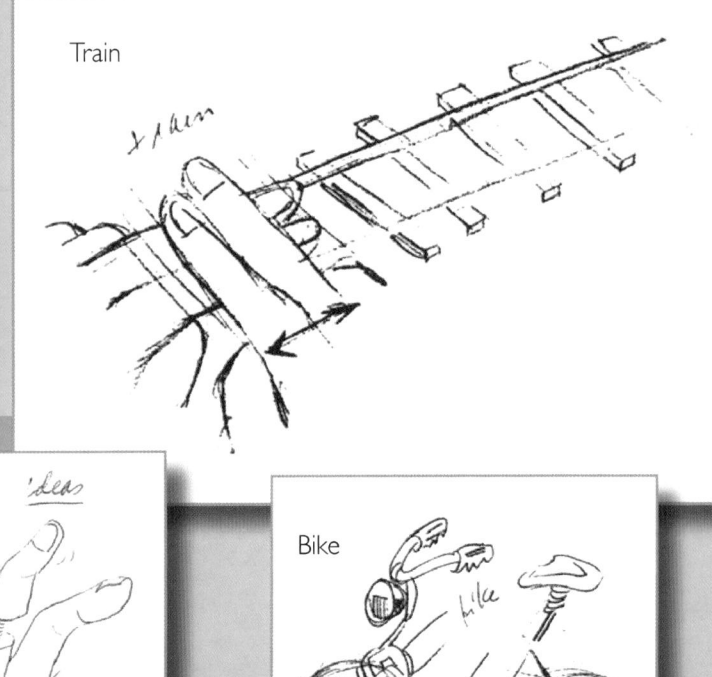

Train

Ideas

Bike

Mirror

SIGNED ART SKETCHES pp. 1 and 2 | 1971
(Selected detail shown throughout chapter).
each 8.5" x 11" (21.6 x 27.9 cm)
graphite and ink on tracing paper
Artist's collection, Seattle

sun feb 6 to fri feb 18, 1972
washburn arts center
gallaudet college   wash dc

art exhibit by
betty g miller

THE SILENT WORLD

OPEN HOUSE SUN FEB 6 & MON FEB 7 FROM 1 TO 5 PM

It is possible that a combination of crab theory and a culture on campus of not supporting students worked together to cause this problem. It is also possible that Miller felt somewhat threatened by these outspoken students. Regardless of the exact mix, the result of this brew was to prevent these students from expressing their art in the way they wanted.

Somewhat ironic is how positive much of Miller's art became in later years. She seemed to fully embrace the DAM concepts after her first volley in a more Dadaist tradition (Note: please see the Introduction for a brief discussion of Dadaism).

▲ THE SILENT WORLD | 1972
8" x 4" (20.3 x 10.2 cm)
ink and letrapress on paper
Artist's collection, Seattle

Three months after Miller's show, Silver graduated from Gallaudet. The Deaf Art Movement looked as if it were growing. Seeds were being spread at the National Technical Institute for the Deaf in Rochester, New York and it was becoming something real. A few years later Miller herself decided to leave Gallaudet and establish a Deaf art colony named *Spectrum: Focus on Deaf Artists* in Texas. Silver was asked to serve on their

Hop-Scotch

Telescope

▲ BRIGHT IDEAS= ANN SILVER | 1972
Harry R. Williams
6.8" x 5.8" x 1.8" (17.3 x 14.7 x 4.6 cm)
oil on canvas inset in wooden frame
Artist's collection, Seattle

Harry R. Williams made this piece for Silver upon her graduation in 1972. When she opened it he explained, "*Your idea bulb is always ON!*" HRW was not generally a Pop Artist, but he made this Deaf Pop Art piece for his friend who was into Pop Art.

The luminescent yellow/orange of the bulb against the blue background makes one feel like the bulb is constantly glowing—no electricity needed.

Note the writing- 72 in the center (for her graduation year) where the wattage would read and his signature arced around the 72— *Harry*, around the top of 72, then *R. Williams* on the lower arc.

"*HRW would sit and tell us stories about artists like the landscape artist and actor Granville Redmond, the sculptor Douglas Tilden and more recent stories of successful Deaf artists like Morris Broderson. I know I didn't know much about any of these artists and I was inspired to know we weren't the first.*

*For as great a place as Gallaudet was, it also left a lot to be desired. The Art Department at that time was far from innovative. We couldn't even put our art up anywhere except on the walls of the classrooms or in one gallery **if** it was approved. We wanted to show the non-art students what we were about. We were thwarted at our every attempt.*

We tried and tried to do what other artists were doing. HRW and I took advantage of our location and visited many of the museums in the DC area. All it did was make us want more. African Americans were able to talk about their experiences. Women were encouraged to express their perspectives on art. When would be OUR time to do the same? That's DAM in a nutshell.

Saddest of all, I'm the only one still alive to tell the tale. All of the main players except me are gone. AIDS and other diseases have taken their toll on Deaf artists of my generation in a serious way. I'm happy to be able to tell this story on behalf of them and for myself too!"

advisory board and did so. The organization Deaf Artists of America was also established in Rochester. There was the beginning of an understanding of what Deaf Art could be.

As Silver lived in DC post-graduation, she and Miller became friends and would have lively discussions about Deaf Art and politics.

Celebration '83 flyer, 1983

Over the next several years, Silver was involved in various gatherings of people from around the world discussing the concept of Deaf Art and the consensus was, regardless of what other terms might be used to describe it, the simplest way to describe the type of art that has a theme inspired by the Deaf experience was simply, *Deaf Art*. An international seminar in Stockholm, Sweden in 1977 confirmed this, as well as one in California in 1983 where Silver was invited to participate along with HRW and John Darcy Smith.

The Deaf Way Festival

Shortly after Dr. I. King Jordan took office as president of Gallaudet University, he supported the concept of a huge world gathering of performers and artists to take place the following year in 1989.

Silver planned to attend the De'VIA workshop by invitation, but a week prior to the first Deaf Way, she had a serious case of mononucleosis and could not be there. She was in constant communication with co-organizers Betty G. Miller and Paul Johnston who carried on a fax dialogue with her amidst their debate and discussions about the name for Deaf Art and the now famous manifesto that came from their deliberations.

Silver has noted that of all the people who were at the discussions at the Deaf Way pre-conference event, only two were in the academic world full time and of the personalities present, it seems unlikely that the term *De'VIA* was created on the spot. It is far more likely that this was a sales pitch made to look like a debate and once again, Betty G. Miller was the likely candidate as the person behind the name *De'VIA* for Deaf Art. Silver believes that if HRW had been alive and at Deaf Way or if she had been able to attend Deaf Way, the term Deaf Art would be the definitive term used for the genre.

The Deaf Art Movement and the term *Deaf Art* have been around since 1968. The term *De'VIA* has been around since 1989. Time will tell which term will survive. They may both survive but *Deaf Art* is still by far the most clear and easy to understand of the two terms.

Chapter 6
DEAF HEART NY

RESERVED AREA ASL INTERPRETING BEGINS this chapter because it represents several events that happened during the time Silver was living in New York (1975-1991). During this time Silver designed logos and she often had reserved seating as a reporter for Silent News. She worked with various museums to promote accessibility and in her spare time she worked as an advocate for Deaf Art.

The white sign with dark green borders and type sits on a forest green background that fades into white. The iconic symbol of an interpreter is in dropout white in a centered bright blue box.

The clever and artistic nature of this piece is lost on some. It looks utilitarian, like an exit sign. If you have seen one, you have seen them all. If you think that, you don't know the whole story. This piece features the mother of all interpreting symbols. It depicts the first interpreting service logo and it was designed by Silver. This piece reserves and immortalizes this logo because it was the first. It is art that quietly pays

homage to her own hard work and, though often overlooked, states for the record that she was here first.

Silver has never been credited, thanked, referenced or recognized for creating the sign language interpreter logo used by hundreds of thousands of people in various countries throughout the world. Let me be the first of many to say that her work is much appreciated.

▲ RESERVED AREA ASL
INTERPRETING | 1992
16" x 20" (40.6 x 50.8 cm)
2-D digital collage
Private collection, Seattle

Why New York?

As a child Silver fantasized about living in the big city of New York—Gotham, as she often calls it. When first meeting her, many people assumed she was a native New Yorker. Perhaps she went to see what perceptions about herself fit people's understanding of a New Yorker.

Here are some more significant reasons she wanted to move to Manhattan in her own words:

"I needed to further my education and immediately enrolled in the M.A. program at New York University.

I sought better career opportunities as an artist and designer that Washington DC could not offer me.

I had a desire to join Gothamites of my ilk in the field of visual/performing arts. Queer artists built the NYC art scene, who else?

I was a foodie before the term was popular. In addition to international cuisine — the U.N. of taste buds, I could not resist Nathan's hot dogs and french fries.

I wanted to enjoy the dizzying array of world-class cultural events around the city. Architecture, museums, large-scale bookstores, year-round film-fests, and the Great White Way (Broadway shows) were a visual feast I could not ignore."

The Gift of a Job...

Upon graduation from New York University in 1977, Silver applied for a job at various firms and was willing to do just about anything. A book publisher was willing to see her work, so she went home and pulled an all-nighter to create eight book cover mock-ups. There were many things she didn't yet know how to do, but her clean hand-lettering work caught the art director's eye. She was immediately hired, though at the bottom of the pay scale. Her job at Ballantine Books was cover design, including layout of the cover, font selection and custom lettering of the book title.

Silver displaying a catalog of book covers she designed, 1980

Close up of GIFT OF LOVE lettering design work, 1978

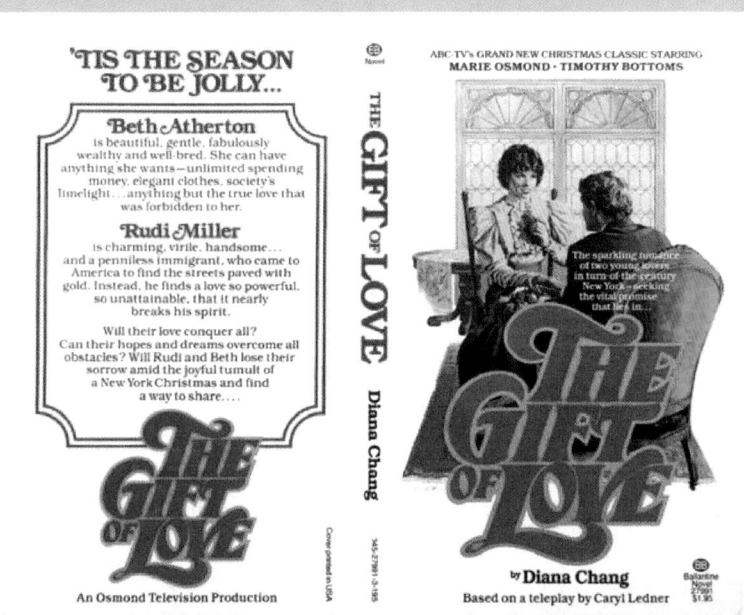

Silver's first published book cover design, 1977

Pink, blue and purple cover versions
(of 8 created), 1977

The Interpreter Logo

Silver worked with the Museum of Modern Art (MoMA) Department of Education and designed the symbol of two hands making the interpreting logo on a background of a triangular shaped body with a round head. Within days of the MoMA's publication of this logo, Silver noticed pirated versions of this same symbol being used with the hands cropped away from the body she set it against- but she could still see the same hands she had created.

The Registry of Interpreters for the Deaf (RID) used a symbol that looks surprisingly similar to this one which they did not copyright for many years because they knew they did not commission its creation.

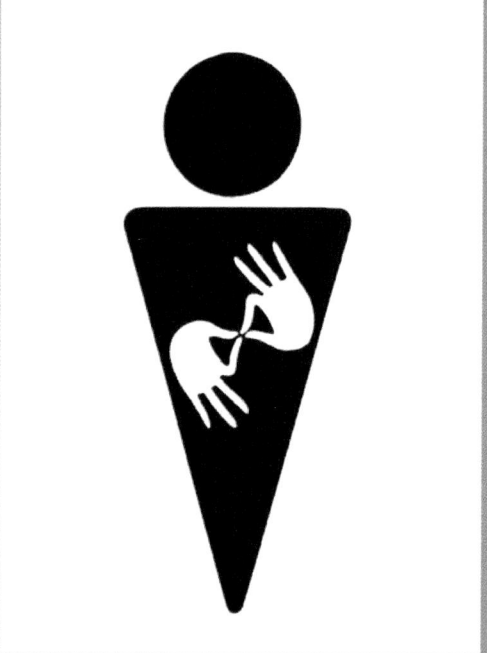

Silver's ASL interpreter symbol, 1979

Examples of Silver's book cover handlettering, 1978-1991

Close up of Silver's handlettering work, 1980

American Association of the
Deaf-Blind, c. 1980

Washington American
Sign Language Teachers
Association, 1999

Deaf AIDS Project, c. 1987

Deaf Logos

With her long experience making book covers, it was logical that Silver branch out and do other graphic design work, including the creation of logos. Silver has won many industry awards and has had her logo designs published in graphic design books highlighting the best of the best. A few samples of her many logo designs are included here.

abused Deaf Women's
Advocacy Services, 2004

Rainbow Alliance of the
Deaf 2001 Conference, 2001

Silversign promotional photo, c. 1989

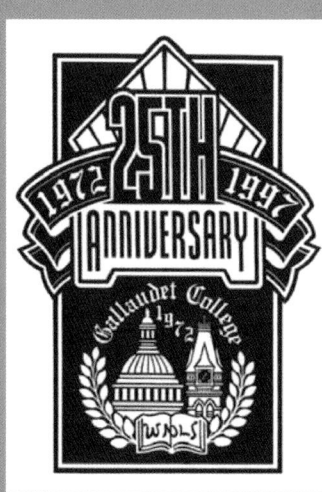

The Bicultural Center, 1993

The 25th Anniversary Reunion
of the Class of 1972 from
Gallaudet University, 1997

DEAF HEART NY

◄ WELL CULTURED, WELL TRAVELED | 1986
11" x 14" (27.9 x 35.6 cm)
Enlarged digital print on paper
Private collection, Chicago

"Cartoons are visual weapons that can get attention for an issue, change people's opinions and get people to confront their prejudices. I love Deaftooning because I can use humor to show something important. I think all Deaf students should try their hand at this. It would help them develop critical thinking skills that are needed more and more these days.

As cultural terminology is one of my favorite subjects, **LABELS** shows how powerful audist tools are to undermine or build up others. In this piece, a hearing man gets a dose of his own medicine."

Photo by: L-J Gilbert

Silver at her desk, 1986

LABELS | 1986 ►
14" x 11" (35.6 x 27.9 cm)
Enlarged digital print on paper
Private collection, Indiana

◀ CHECKERED HAPPY
NEW YEAR | 2005
6.2" x 5" (15.7 x 12.7 cm)
Ink on paper greeting card
Artist's collection, Seattle

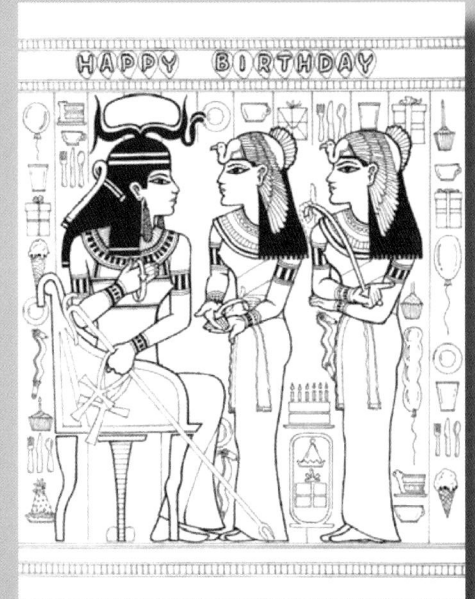

EGYPTIAN BIRTHDAY | 1985 ▶
6" x 8.4" (15.2 x 21.3 cm)
Ink on paper greeting card
Artist's collection, Seattle

◀ ULTIMATE NEW
YEAR CARD | 1993
5" x 6.5" (12.7 x 16.5 cm)
Ink on paper greeting card
Artist's collection, Seattle

VISHNU BIRTHDAY | 1985 ▶
6" x 8.4" (15.2 x 21.3 cm)
Ink on paper greeting card
Artist's collection, Seattle

SUBWAY NEW YEAR | 1982 ▼
9.25" x 4" (23.5 x 10.1 cm)
Ink on paper greeting card
Artist's collection, Seattle

The ILY Sign Book Project

In the mid-1970s, Silver had an idea for a book. She thought it would be interesting to collect photographs of various people signing the I-Love-You sign/gesture in ASL. During the early 1980s, she approached several publishing houses but for one reason or another, no one was willing to publish it. Some said it was not marketable, some said it was not interesting enough, and some rejected it without giving any feedback whatsoever. Before approaching anyone about publishing her idea, Silver had collected hundreds of ILY sign photographs of well known celebrities, authors, dignitaries, soldiers, artists and international figures. Her position as a reporter for *Silent News* gave her a press pass and access to some people she wouldn't have met otherwise. Most were very gracious and very happy to comply. Some expected money up front, which Silver was not willing or able to pay and a few turned her down flat. Nonetheless, she continued to take ILY sign photos through the late 1990s.

"I seriously regret not having the idea for the ILY book soon enough to get an ILY sign photo of Andy Warhol, but I am very happy with the many excellent photos I have of people like LeRoy Neiman, Harrison Ford, Muhammad Ali, Meryl Streep, Oliver Sacks, Harvey Fierstein, Mayor Ed Koch, Senator Tom Harkin, Gene Wilder and Tetsuko Kuroyanagi of Japan. I have too many photos to mention here! Perhaps someday I will be able to get them published..."

Artist LeRoy Neiman, 1988

Author Oliver Sacks, 1989

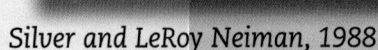

Silver and LeRoy Neiman, 1988

Senator Tom Harkin, 1988

Actress/TV show host Tetsuko (Totto-chan)
Kuroyanagi in full kimono, 1987

Actor Gene Wilder,
1983

NYC Mayor Edward Koch, 1984

Actor and playwright
Harvey Fierstein, 1980

Silver and Gene Wilder, 1983

61

Chapter 7

FAN OF JAPAN

SILVER'S INTEREST IN THINGS JAPANESE started at a young age. When she was a small child she was taken to the Seattle Asian Art Museum from time to time where she was exposed to a variety of Japanese and other Asian cultural artifacts. Her family would occasionally shop at Uwajimaya, one of the largest Asian grocery retailers in the Pacific Northwest. Shopping there is a cultural experience, and a weekly tradition for Silver today.

Growing up, Silver's father often took the family to the Hong Kong Restaurant for dinner on Sundays. Over the years she cultivated a fondness for Chinese cuisine and mastered the chopsticks.

Expressing **Happy New Year** in five ways, this original greeting card includes it in two written forms of Japanese on the wall. It is written in English on the open pages and depicted in ASL as well. The fact that the lady is looking away from the viewer allows for a much more careful examination of the bright red kimono dropped low off her bare back in restrained sensuality. Looking closely, one sees the fifth way is in Japanese Sign Language (JSL), amid the waves tattooed on her back.

▲ THE TATTOOED LADY *(from 1987 card)* │ 2012
11" x 14" (27.9 x 35.6 cm)
Enlarged digital print on paper
Private collection, Chicago

The Fellowship

All her life, Silver wanted to fulfill her dream of visiting Japan. In 1985 she decided to apply for a National Endowment for the Arts (NEA) grant. She was a finalist, based on some written materials but mostly for 10 pieces she made that pertained to Japanese culture from a Deaf perspective. Her art caught the eye of several on the review committee who passed on her application to the Japan-U.S. Friendship Commission. This commission also loved her work and gave her a fellowship to fully support the program she outlined of a nine-month stay in Japan teaching about Deaf culture, encouraging the development of Deaf

Silver (center) with grandmother, siblings & cousin at the museum, 1956

Silver (right) with siblings and cousin at the Seattle Asian Art Museum, 1956

When she attended Gallaudet, she never missed an opportunity to paint or draw something Asian related. Once a model came to class in a sarong which she depicted in oil pastel.

WOMAN IN ANIMAL SARONG | 1970 ▶
18" x 24" (45.7 x 60.9 cm)
oil pastel on paper
Artist's collection, Seattle

▲ CHI | 1985
10" x 10" (25.4 x 25.4 cm)
watercolor and marker on paper
Artist's collection, Seattle

history preservation and demonstrating how political change is possible for Deaf people.

She would say later that she was there on a Deaf "safari." She met a Deaf Japanese couple who invited her to stay with them in Nakano. That was a big benefit to her work because they put her in contact with the right people to help accomplish her goals.

While she was there she learned many things about Japanese culture. Aside from a serious problem with a translation of one term she used, there were other subtle things in her artwork that she did not realize she was communicating through the choices she had made in

her art. Japanese culture ascribes a set of meanings to various conditions in a piece of art.

Today most Japanese people and many younger Americans are familiar with this concept conveyed via Japanese manga (animé) iconography. Silver was unaware of it when she was preparing her art for submission. She depicts a few of the women with loose strands of hair and kimonos that are loose around the neck. These two things together represent a woman who has recently had sex or someone who was caught while having sex. *ARUFABETTO - ALPHABET, CHI, GASSHŪKOKU - USA,* and to some extent, *INTERPRETER IN GREEN KIMONO* all exhibit this. To a trained eye, these mean *I Study the Alphabet After Sex, Fingerspelling Turns Me On, ASL is Hot,* and *The Interpreter in the Green Kimono is Promiscuous.* This artwork has not been on display since Silver returned from Japan in 1986 until now. The inclusion in this section is

◀ ARUFABETTO - ALPHABET | 1985
10" x 10" (25.4 x 25.4 cm)
watercolor and
marker on paper
Artist's collection, Seattle

Careful Who You Ask!

"As I was preparing to complete artwork submission for my fellowship application, I needed an English-to-Japanese translator. I lived in New York, the most cosmopolitan city in the country. I found a Japanese man on the street and asked him if he would translate a few words into Kanji for me. The stranger happily complied. Looking back, that was quite a mistake. I had no idea what this man's educational background was or his ability with Kanji. Most importantly I was to learn later, I also didn't know about his cultural biases toward Deaf people.

When I received the grant and traveled to Japan, I learned by the shocked faces and disapproving looks that my street-chosen translator had taken the English word deaf as the Japanese equal to the term deaf and dumb. The term in Japan is equally as offensive to Deaf people there as it is here, and I unwittingly let my artwork hold that label! My humblest apologies to all Deaf Japanese people."

not meant to be offensive, but to show how an American artist won a fellowship from an American panel who screened artwork entries that conveyed these messages– yet no one along the way, including the artist, knew the messages these pieces actually contained.

▲ TSUNBO-NO / DEAF (not) | 1985
10" x 10" (25.4 x 25.4 cm)
watercolor and marker on paper
Artist's collection, Seattle

Note: In this piece Silver depicts the dictionary she had illustrated while working in New York.

▲ GASSHŪKOKU - USA | 1985
10" x 10" (25.4 x 25.4 cm)
watercolor and marker on paper
Artist's collection, Seattle

67

Silver appeared twice on NHK-TV in Japan, 1986

◀ NIPPON - JAPAN
10" x 10" (25.4 x 25.4 cm)
watercolor and
marker on paper
Artist's collection, Seattle

▲ INTERPRETER IN GREEN KIMONO | 1985
10" x 10" (25.4 x 25.4 cm)
watercolor and marker on paper
Artist's collection, Seattle

A contemplative moment from the window of Silver's residence in Nakano, Japan, 1986

Silver flashes an American fan during a lecture in Tokyo, Japan, 1986

69

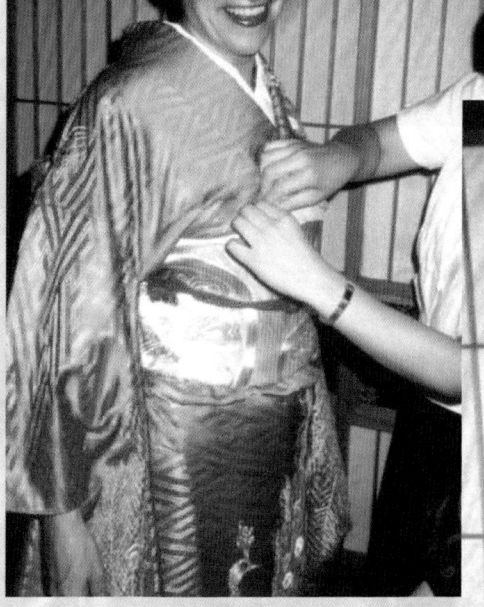

Silver dressing, 1986

Authentic Kimono

Silver was given a great honor while she was in Japan. As a Westerner, she was allowed to be dressed in traditional Japanese kimono.

Silver in full formal kimono, 1986

▲ SŪ / NUMBERS | 1985
10" x 10" (25.4 x 25.4 cm)
watercolor and marker on paper
Artist's collection, Seattle

71

DENTATSU /
COMMUNICATION | 1985 ▶
10" x 10" (25.4 x 25.4 cm)
watercolor and marker on paper
Artist's collection, Seattle

◀ JAPAN-USA
GOOD FELLOWSHIP | 1985
10" x 10" (25.4 x 25.4 cm)
watercolor and marker on paper
Artist's collection, Seattle

▲ AI / ILY | 1985
10" × 10" (25.4 x 25.4 cm)
watercolor and marker on paper
Artist's collection, Seattle

KABUKI NEW YEAR | 1985 ▲
11.1" x 4.75" (28.2 x 12 cm)
Ink on paper greeting card
Artist's collection, Seattle

▲ **THE FOUR BUDDHAS** *(from 1989 card)* | 2012
11" x 14" (27.9 x 35.6 cm)
Enlarged digital print on paper
Artist's collection, Seattle

AKEMASHITE OMEDETOH GOZAIMASU

▲ **JSL NEW YEAR** | 1987
5" x 7" (12.7 x 17.8 cm)
Ink on paper greeting card
Artist's collection, Seattle

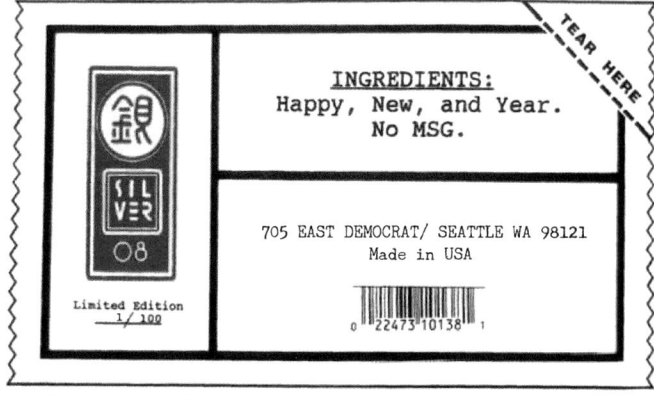

◀ JOY SAUCE | 2008　(reverse of card) ▲
7" x 4" (17.8 x 10.2 cm)
Ink on paper limited edition greeting card
Artist's collection, Seattle

At **Ann Silver:
ONE WAY,
DEAF WAY—
The Solo Show** in
April 2012, there
was great interest
in enlarged prints
of limited edition
greeting cards from
various years past.

◀WOODCUT GEISHAS
(from 2006 card) | 2012
11" x 14" (27.9 x 35.6 cm)
Enlarged digital print on paper
Private collection, Chicago

Silver giving one of many presentations in Japan on American Deaf culture, 1986

Silver and Yutaka Osugi, 1986

Silver Geisha, 1986

Samurai Silver! 1986

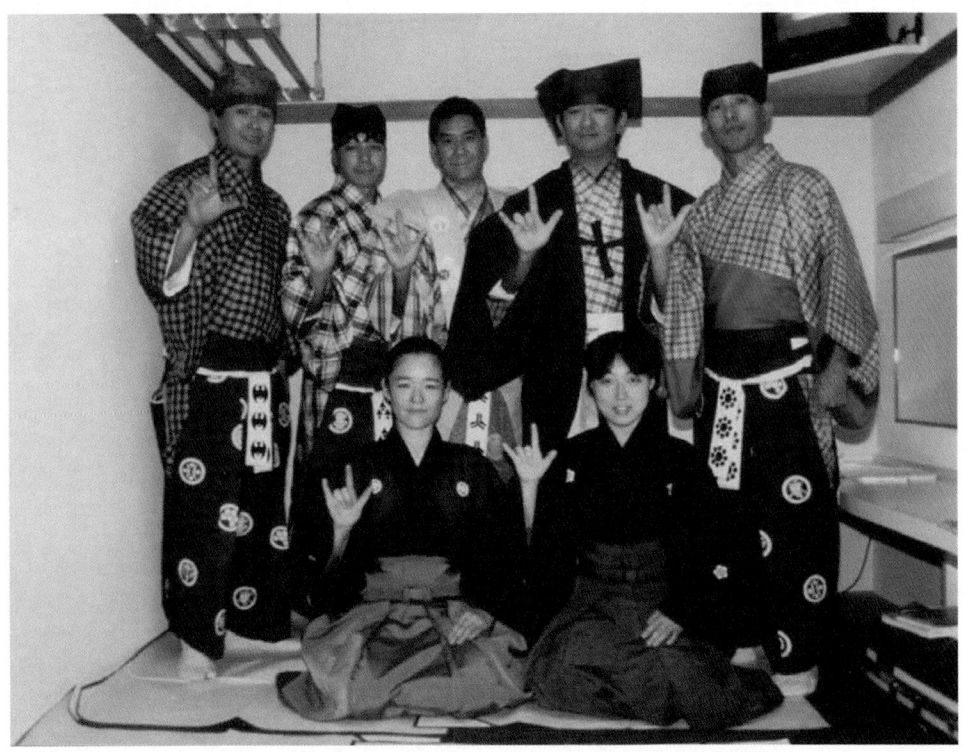

Japanese Theatre of the Deaf, 1986

Photo: The Japan Times, Ltd.

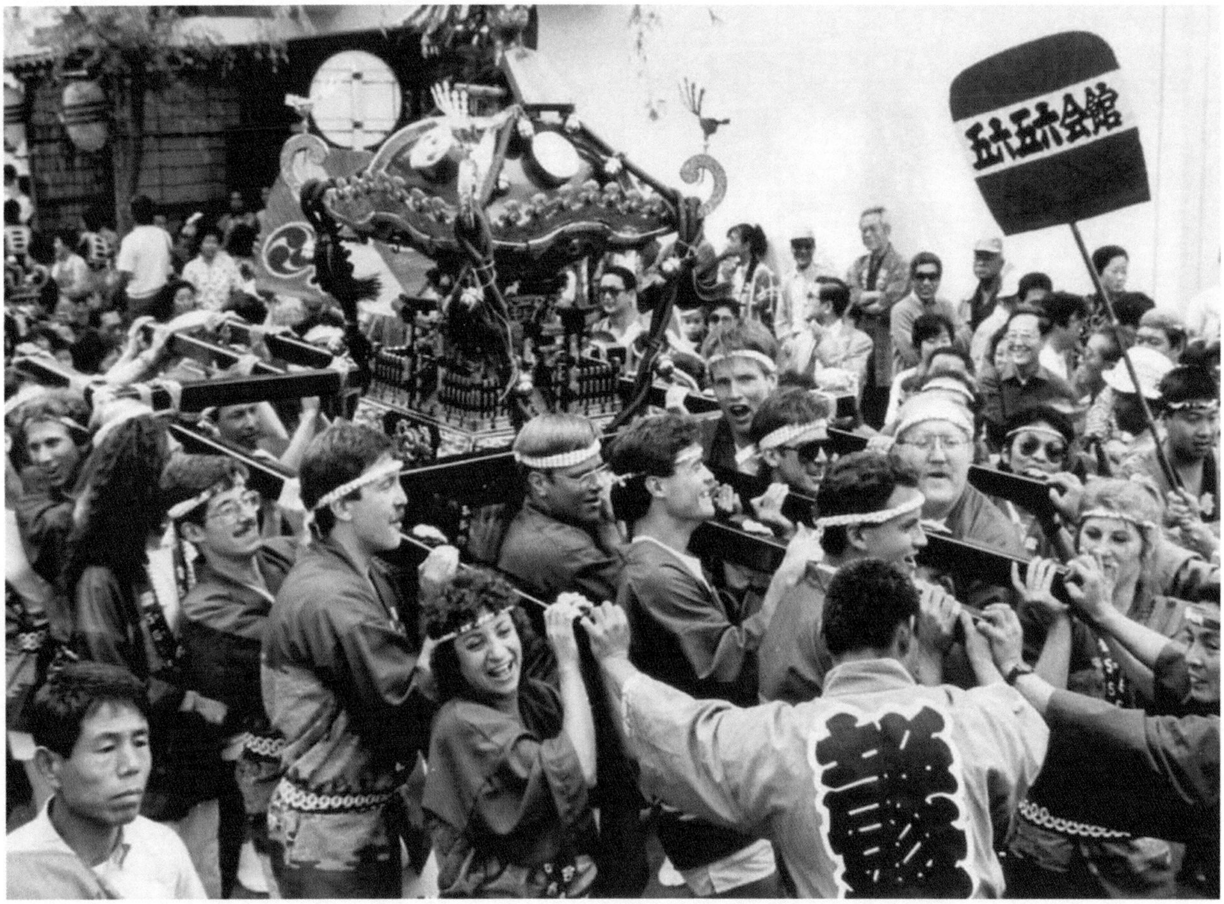

Silver (bottom center) helps to carry a mikoshi (portable shrine) during the Sanja Festival, 1986

▲ TBC NEWS IS CHEAP
IN ANY LANGUAGE | 1992
10" x 8" (25.4 x 20.3 cm)
Ink on paper
Artist's collection, Seattle

Silver's Deaf Buddha collection, 2012

Silver's sushi passion, 1986

JSL SAYONARA | 1988 ▲
(Papermill Playhouse [NJ] theatre playbill artwork only)
7" x 4" (17.8 x 10.2 cm)
Ink on paper
Artist's collection, Seattle

HOMAGE TO DEAF WOMEN
OF AMERICA *(self-portrait)* | 1981 ▶
18" x 24" (45.7 x 60.9 cm)
colored pencil, ink and letrapress on paper
Artist's collection, Seattle

HOMAGE TO DEAF WOMEN OF AMERICA

ANN SILVER
1981

Chapter 8
DEAF PRESIDENT NOW

IN THE SPRING OF 1988, THE BOARD OF Trustees of Gallaudet University, the only liberal arts university that was designed specifically for the needs of Deaf students, had the opportunity to make history. They had three candidates for the position of President of the university-- two men, both Deaf and well respected educators and one hearing woman who knew no Deaf people and who could not sign. The campus community made it known to the Board that they expected a Deaf person to be selected as President. Jane Bassett Spilman, grand-daughter of the founder of Bassett Furniture and wife of the president of the company, had served on the Gallaudet University Board of Trustees for many years but had never learned about Deaf culture or learned the language of the students who attended the University.

JOIN GALLAUDET | 1988 ▲
10" x 8" (25.4 x 20.3 cm)
Ink on paper
Artist's collection, Seattle

▲ PAH Est. 1988 | 1993
16" x 20" (40.6 x 50.8 cm)
2-D layered paper collage
Private collection, Massachusetts

81

Spilman is known for saying, *"Deaf people are not ready to function in a hearing world."* Although she claimed to have never actually said this, blaming a poor interpretation of her words.

When she announced that the Board of Trustees had selected Dr. Elizabeth Zinser as the president of Gallaudet University, a series of events began that have since become known as the Deaf President Now (DPN) Movement. Students, faculty, staff and supporters banded together with a united front never seen until that time in the Deaf community for the single cause of the selection of a Deaf president. It was an easy concept to understand, and made for a good sound byte for the media.

After a long week of protests, on March 13, 1988, the Board did select Dr. I. King Jordan as the first Deaf president in Gallaudet's history.

Silver created a series of Deaftoons about the various events happening at her alma mater from her vantage point in New York City. She captured many of the sentiments of the protesters with her succinct prose and witty and heartfelt illustrations. Several of these found their way into publications including **TBC News** and Jack Gannon's book, **The Week the World Heard Gallaudet**. Silver's DPN-related Deaftoons tell a visual story of the events of the historic protest that changed the Deaf community and Deaf culture forever.

*"It can't be just a coincidence.
My alphabet soup is spelling out only 'D', 'P', and 'N'."*

DPN ALPHABET SOUP | 1993 ▲
10" x 8" (25.4 x 20.3 cm)
Ink on paper
Artist's collection, Seattle

THE FOUR DEMANDMENTS | 1988 ▶
8" x 10" (20.3 x 25.4 cm)
Ink on paper
Artist's collection, Seattle

DPN Deaftoons

◀ COIN TOSS VOTING | 1988
10" x 8" (25.4 x 20.3 cm)
Ink on paper
Artist's collection, Seattle

RAY'S PIZZA | 1988 ▲
10" x 8" (25.4 x 20.3 cm)
Ink on paper
Artist's collection, Seattle

DR. ZINSER GETS A T-SHIRT | 1988 ▲
10" x 8" (25.4 x 20.3 cm)
Ink on paper
Artist's collection, Seattle

VICTORY | 1988 ▶
8" x 10" (20.3 x 25.4 cm)
Ink on paper
Artist's collection, Seattle

10" x 8" (25.4 x 20.3 cm)
Ink on paper
Artist's collection, Seattle

Clayton Valli

Clayton Valli was an ASL poet who was also a professor in the Linguistics Department at Gallaudet University. He was the first person to ever earn a Ph.D. in ASL Poetry in 1993.

Before earning his doctorate, he and Silver became friends. They visited each other from time to time, and Clayton inspired Silver regarding her desire to continue her education. Silver enrolled at the same college from which Clayton was graduated and took classes for two years toward a Ph.D. in Deaf Art. They shared the same birthday and sent annual birthday faxes to one another from the time they met until his untimely death in 2003. One of the books

Clayton Valli receives Silver's art given to him by friends, 1993

Clayton and Silver in a photo booth, 1992

Clayton authored was about the sign 'PAH' which he made well known via his use of the sign and the book and video which showed what the sign meant to various Deaf people. The written symbol 'PAH' is a literal interpretation of the mouth activity made when producing the sign that means "At long last!" The commissioned artwork refers to the Deaf President Now Movement of 1988. After 124 years, PAH! Gallaudet University finally had a Deaf president.

"We find the defendant guilty as charged.
We sentence him to read Jack Gannon's book titled
The Week The World Heard Gallaudet."

DEAF PREZ NOW WIND-UP TOYS | 1988 ▲
10" x 8" (25.4 x 20.3 cm)
Ink on paper
Artist's collection, Seattle

*"That's your Grandma Zinser who perished
in the Gallaudet Stampede of '88."*

▲ GALLAUDET STAMPEDE | 1988
8" x 10" (20.3 x 25.4 cm)
Ink on paper
Artist's collection, Seattle

"This is Ryan's first protest."

▲ RYAN'S FIRST PROTEST | 1988
8" x 10" (20.3 x 25.4 cm)
Ink on paper
Artist's collection, Seattle

*"Which would you like—
the King Jordan wind-up toy, the Jane Spilman eraser,
or the Elisabeth Zinser disappearing ink?"*

◄ 5th ANNIVERSARY OF DPN | 1993
8" x 10" (20.3 x 25.4 cm)
Ink on paper
Artist's collection, Seattle

I WANT HIM TO BE
DEAF PRESIDENT | 1988 ▶
10" x 8" (25.4 x 20.3 cm)
Ink on paper
Artist's collection, Seattle

GALLAUDET UNIVERSITY
LIVED HAPPILY
EVER AFTER | 1988 ▶
10" x 8" (25.4 x 20.3 cm)
Ink on paper
Artist's collection, Seattle

"...and on March 13th-- 124 years later,
Gallaudet University lived happily ever after."

"His father wants him to be a lawyer,
but I want him to be Deaf president of Gallaudet University."

Dr. I. King Jordan

DEAF PEOPLE CAN DO ANYTHING | 1993 ▶
20" x 16" (50.8 x 40.6 cm)
2-D layered paper collage
Private collection, Virginia

Dr. Jordan and Silver shake hands, 1988

First appearance of Dr. Jordan's quote from Silver's article on cover of **Silent News** *(Vol. 20, No. 4, 1988)*

From Silver's base in New York City, she had a side job of working as an editor and reporter for **Silent News**. Immediately after Dr. I. King Jordan became president she interviewed him for a feature story. Silver captured his quote "Deaf people can do anything except hear" for the cover of **Silent News**. This may have been the first time the quote was in print. She attended his inaugural presidential address in which he also used the famous quote in his speech.

Dr. Jordan and his wife Linda have been friends with Silver since college days. Linda Jordan was a strong advocate for Deaf Art throughout Dr. Jordan's presidency.

DEAF PEOPLE CAN DO ANYTHING EXCEPT...

HEARING PEOPLE CAN DO ANYTHING EXCEPT...

Reminding one of a grassy field that succumbs to a sunny horizon, the green backdrop on this piece could be anywhere. Two blue framed white signs stand on posts, nearly identical to each other. The first states that **DEAF PEOPLE CAN DO ANYTHING EXCEPT...** and the second points out the corollary fact, **HEARING PEOPLE CAN DO ANYTHING EXCEPT...**

This piece is based on a saying that Dr. Jordan said soon after taking office in 1988. His original quote was: Deaf people can do anything except hear. Silver wanted to point out the injustice with limiting Deaf people, when hearing people have many limitations as well.

About three years after this piece was created, Dr. Jordan was retelling an anecdote about his son having a license plate cover with his original quote on it. The upper portion of the cover said, Deaf People Can Do Anything and the lower portion said Except Hear. Over time, the plate happened to break in half. When he had recently seen his son, he noticed that the lower portion of the license plate holder had fallen off, leaving only the statement, Deaf People can Do Anything— which Dr. Jordan promoted as a more positive spin-off of his original quote.

Chapter 9
Mmm Mmm DEAF

OF THE MOST ICONIC OF SILVER'S WORK and one that became an instant classic, this box of laundry soap offers to wash all the cares and worries of the hearing world away if one only has an ample amount of **DEAF PRIDE**. This piece starts with a white background and a bright orange three-dimensional-looking box pops off the page with its

KENDALL'S ASL, ENGLISH & BI-BI FLAKES | 1992 ▲
20" x 16" (50.8 x 40.6 cm)
2-D layered paper collage
Private collection, Seattle

strong advertising slogan: **IF IT'S GOT TO BE SIGN LANGUAGE, IT'S GOT TO BE ASL.**

IF IT'S GOT TO BE SIGN LANGUAGE, Deaf Pride IT'S GOT TO BE ASL.

1/5   Silver '99

▲ DEAF PRIDE | 1999
20" x 16" (50.8 x 40.6 cm)
2-D layered paper collage
Private collection, Georgia

(next page)
A CENTURY OF DIFFERENCE | 2002 ▶
20" x 16" (50.8 x 40.6 cm)
2-D layered paper collage
Private collection, Texas

DEAF&DUMB 1900

HANDICAPPED 19 40

DISABLED 1980

AP 6/10

DEAF-MUTE
1920

HEARING
IMPAIRED
1960

DEAF
2000

Silver '02

Come a Long Way?

While it can be said that Deaf people have come a long way since the last turn of the century, societal audism (prejudice against Deaf culture) has made the struggle a difficult one. Terminology used by hearing people for labeling Deaf people rarely has fit what Deaf people want to call themselves. In the piece A CENTURY OF DIFFERENCE, on the previous page, the six red, white and blue license plates play off each other, using different fonts and layouts for each plate so that each double-decade depicted has its own identity.

The white with red outlined plate, DEAF & DUMB 1900 starts the piece with a hand-made font and a drop shadow line often seen in products of that era. Next is DEAF-MUTE 1920 using a stylized Gatsbian font on a white-outlined royal blue plate with red-outlined white lettering and a flow reminiscent of French advertising posters of that time.

Starting the middle set, the plate perfectly captures the World War II and Korean War driven double-decade with the double white-outlined blue plate, HANDICAPPED 1940. Silver uses a militaristic stencil font in sprayed-on white with the 19 and 40 in red, separated and on two white gun sight circles on a red rectangle. Following this is HEARING IMPAIRED 1960 using minimalist design. It is a white plate outlined in red and blue with IMPAIRED stretched over a red rectangle consuming the plate. The changing double-decade is depicted with a minimum of fuss.

The last set starts with DISABLED 1980, a disjointed and fragmented plate using opposing blue and red backgrounds and font colors with a typewriter-style font separating DIS and ABLED, once again perfectly reflecting the fragmented goals and styles of this double-decade. Silver finishes with the red, white and blue flag-like plate DEAF 2000. She uses white stars on a blue field crossing the top portion of the plate with red stripes crossing and curving on the white field with DEAF in patriotic blue and 2000 in flag-waving red. Added to all this is a hammered gun-metal gray background giving the piece a firm ground from which to shine.

One might take the year of each plate and if a hearing person was born around that year, the term on the license plate is likely how that person was culturally trained to see and understand Deaf people. We may be improving, but are we truly there yet?

> "Labels reflect how we view the world, others and ourselves. Words, beliefs and assumptions that are stereotypical, patronizing and demeaning limit the ways in which people perceive each other and their choices. Because medical viewpoints have successfully prevented us from being classed as a true linguistic and cultural minority, negative labels are still tolerated in the dominant culture's language and literature."

DEAF & DUMB 1903 / DEAF 1993 | 1993 ▶
16" x 20" (40.6 x 50.8 cm)
2-D layered paper collage
Private collection, West Virginia

Silver '93

(previous page)
DEAF IDENTITY CRAYONS:
Then & Now | 1999
20" x 16" (50.8 x 40.6 cm)
2-D layered paper collage
Private collection, New Hampshire

(describing artwork on previous page)
From a distance the observer sees a field of green and two boxes of crayons, one old and one new. Upon closer inspection, one sees the vintage box is filled with old and misguided identity terms. The modern box is filled with more recent and more positive identity terms for the Deaf community.

"A century ago, Deaf people were no more than a box of crayons. We have seen changes in terms during the 20th century, but the removal of the power of these belittling and hurtful words on our community is far from over. We can't let others define who we are. We are completely capable of determining what we should be called."

"Here is my take on the two crayons I get asked about the most:

*The SEEING crayon is a tribute to the late John Darcy Smith, one of the proponents of the Deaf Art Movement. During the Sixties, he waged an unsuccessful word-conversion campaign at a time when political correctness had not become fashionable. His reasoning for the term was that if humans who depend on sound are called **hearing** people, others who rely on sight should likewise be labeled **seeing** rather than the much more negative term **hearing-impaired**. We are **SEEING** people!*

The CODA crayon represents a child (offspring) of a Deaf Adult (more commonly called Deaf parents). If a person is raised in a community by its members, like it or not, that person is a part of that community. They may reject or embrace the identity they have been given so their exact place in the community is up to them, but CODAs are a part of the Deaf community. To think otherwise is ridiculous."

John Darcy Smith

John Darcy Smith, 1985

PROGRESS SOUP:
Manual Alphabet | 1992 ▶
16" x 20" (40.6 x 50.8 cm)
2-D layered paper collage
Private collection, Ontario, Canada

Silver '92

Andy Warhol

For nearly the entire time Silver was in New York, she lived in Andy Warhol's neighborhood. Silver was surprised to learn that they were attending the same parties. She was touched that she was recognized by Warhol enough to be personally invited to parties he hosted although she would never claim that she was much more than an acquaintance of Andy's.

Silver had been familiar with his art which appeared on magazine covers when she was in high school. She was always keenly interested in the Pop Art movement as it was happening, but her time to do artwork was overly limited during her time in New York. She was unable to explore her own interpretation of this movement—Deaf Pop Art, until the 1990s.

Ann Silver with arm around Andy Warhol, 1983 (Notice the look of tolerant amusement on his face.)

This piece is somewhat of an homage to her friend Warhol. On a tan graduated background, Silver builds images of five soup cans that feed the mind. She uses the Gallaudet University logo as the medallion and brands each one with the Gallaudet name. She includes Deaf Culture, ASL, Deaf Art/ De'VIA & Deaf History as the four food groups supporting the jumbo-sized can of Deaf Studies.

"Whenever I'd run into Warhol in my neighborhood, at Max's Kansas City, at Studio 54 or elsewhere, he'd always have a tape recorder in his hand and at times a camera (a Polaroid, I'd swear).

One of his friends told me that he didn't like eye contact. I felt this odd since he and I always had full eye contact because he was obviously sensitive to my communication needs.

Unbeknownst to me, Warhol's closest friends cringed at the sight of my putting my arm around Warhol or hugging him. He seemed to take it in stride from me. Again, perhaps because of me being his Deaf friend in the neighborhood, he gave me more leeway than he would accept from others, or at least that is how I choose to remember him..."

▲ GALLAUDET'S DEAF STUDIES SOUP GROUP | 1992
20" x 16" (50.8 x 40.6 cm)
2-D layered paper collage
Collection, Gallaudet University

(next page)
WILL THE REAL GOYA PLEASE STAND UP? | 1996 ▶
20" x 16" (50.8 x 40.6 cm)
2-D layered paper collage
Private collection, Louisiana

FRANCISCO DE GOYA Y LUCIENTES

DARK SIDE OF HUMAN NATURE

OLD

history/genre painter, printmaker, caricaturist, church decorator, tapestry designer, portraitist, aficionado of the fantastic, and Painter-in-Chief to the King of Spain

K

EL SORDO ARTE

NET WEIGHT 16 OZ. (454g)

"THE DISASTERS OF <u>E</u> WAR"

Francisco de Goya y Lucientes (1746-1828)

GOYA
was an artist

GOYA
was deaf

GOYA
was an artist who happened to be deaf

GOYA
was an artist and deaf

GOYA
was a deaf artist

GOYA
was deaf and an artist

GOYA
was an artist formerly hearing

*W*ill the real Goya please stand up?

0 41196 01015 2

Will the Real Goya Please Stand Up?

On the previous pages, two sides of a bright blue and yellow can float on a faded ivory background. This piece makes many statements about the artist and raises many questions for the viewer.

If one wishes to categorize Goya, what lens will he or she use to do so? If he were alive today would he label his own work Deaf Art? There is a cautionary tale in this piece. Just because an artist is audiologically deaf does not mean that all of their artwork is Deaf Art. On the other hand, some artists who are deaf deny that their work relates in any way or was influenced by their life as a deaf person, when most art consumers can easily see a connection to their artwork and being Deaf. Does work within a genre such as Deaf Art require the consent of the artist? This seems absurd.

It would be equally absurd, however, to give extra praise for the work of a Deaf artist because he or she "overcame" their nature as a deaf person by becoming successful. This is faulty logic. If a woman has blue eyes, she does not overcome this by making money. It would be more appropriate to say that she overcame being a stereotypical starving artist by becoming successful. If she decides to wear brown contact lenses, she has not overcome her blue eyes. She is simply hiding her true nature.

Taking this a step further, if she became successful using blue paint in her work, does the use of this color automatically refer to the true nature of her eyes? What if she wishes to convey a realistic sky? Must that be eye-color related? If we learned that Picasso had blue eyes that he somehow changed to appear brown, would that change our perception of his *blue* period? Would that now make him an automatic part of a latter cultural and political decision to create a blue genre of art?

I have heard that many artists who are asked to act as jurists for art exhibits featuring Deaf Art or deaf artists decline because they feel they have no basis on which to evaluate the work of the subject artists. This is a cop out at best.

Color, composition, texture, process, and technique are always going to be a part of the work of an artist. These factors can be evaluated on their own merit or lack thereof.

Artists like Silver have taken a stand with a desire to have their work be part of a genre of Deaf Art. She has made it very clear in her work and in her life that her nature is reflected in her work. This does not mean, however, that one cannot use another lens to see her work and how it compares to that of others.

As for **WILL THE REAL GOYA PLEASE STAND UP?,** that depends on the viewer's lens. The real Goya is always there in his work and will be there as long as the art is visible, regardless of which lens the viewer uses to see him. In the same way, the real Silver is always there in her work too.

The bigger question may be– if you only see Silver as a person who is deaf, can you see all that her art has to offer you?

PREPARATION HH | 1996 ▲
20" x 16" (50.8 x 40.6 cm)
2-D layered paper collage
Private collection, Seattle

Barbara Kannapell

Dr. Barbara Kannapell attended the Indiana School for the Deaf and graduated from Gallaudet in 1961. She co-founded the organization Deafpride in 1972 and obtained her Ph.D. in sociolinguistics with an emphasis on the community and identity of Deaf people. She has presented widely on topics of Deaf culture and sociolinguistics and emphasizes the importance of bi-lingual education for Deaf children. Kanny, as she is known to her friends, and Silver have known each other for many years.

Silver and Barbara Kannapell, 1992

Deaf with a capital D

In this book, the reader may notice the word Deaf is often spelled with a capital **D**. This is now a common signifier in books related to Deaf culture and ASL. Capital **D (Deaf)** refers to people who are associated with Deaf culture or in some way refers to Deaf culture. The use of lowercase **d (deaf)** pertains to audiological status only. In recent years, authors of books pertaining to Deaf people and Deaf culture, authors err on the side of the use of capital **Deaf** rather than **deaf**.

This three-dimensional-looking **Special D** cereal box floats on a blue gradient background. The tan hand depicting the fingerspelled D looks striking against the white box and large green D behind it. **Kendall** is the name of the campus of Gallaudet University (Kendall Green) because the first school there was originally owned and established by the 8th Postmaster General, Amos Kendall, in 1857.

In essence, this piece is saying that Gallaudet University is the place that contains the kernels of **Deaf with a capital D** culture.

KENDALL'S SPECIAL D | 1999 ▶
16" x 20" (40.6 x 50.8 cm)
2-D layered paper collage
Private collection, Tennessee

Marilyn Jean Smith

Silver and Marilyn Smith, 2006

As Seattle natives and friends for over half a century, Smith and Silver each made their mark on the world. Marilyn has been and continues to be honored for her pioneering work as the founder and retired Executive Director of abused Deaf Women's Advocacy Services. Many cities around the country have followed this model to provide similar services.

Marilyn's return to their mutual birthplace of Seattle some two decades after graduation from their alma mater had such an impact, Silver decided to do the same soon after. Is there something in the Seattle water that made them both agents of change?

"Throughout elementary school years together, Marilyn mistook me for a Native-American, judging from my summer-tanned skin and long braids."

"Whenever I eat out, hearing people, like the maitre d' for instance, often have difficulty understanding me when I use my voice to speak my name. To reserve my place, I usually say 'Marilyn Smith' instead of my own name as an easy way out.

As an exquisite chef and the hostess with the mostest, Marilyn is viewed by many as the Deaf Martha Stewart."

ADWAS /
MARILYN SMITH'S COOKERY | 1996 ▶
16" x 20" (40.6 x 50.8 cm)
2-D layered paper collage
Private collection, Seattle

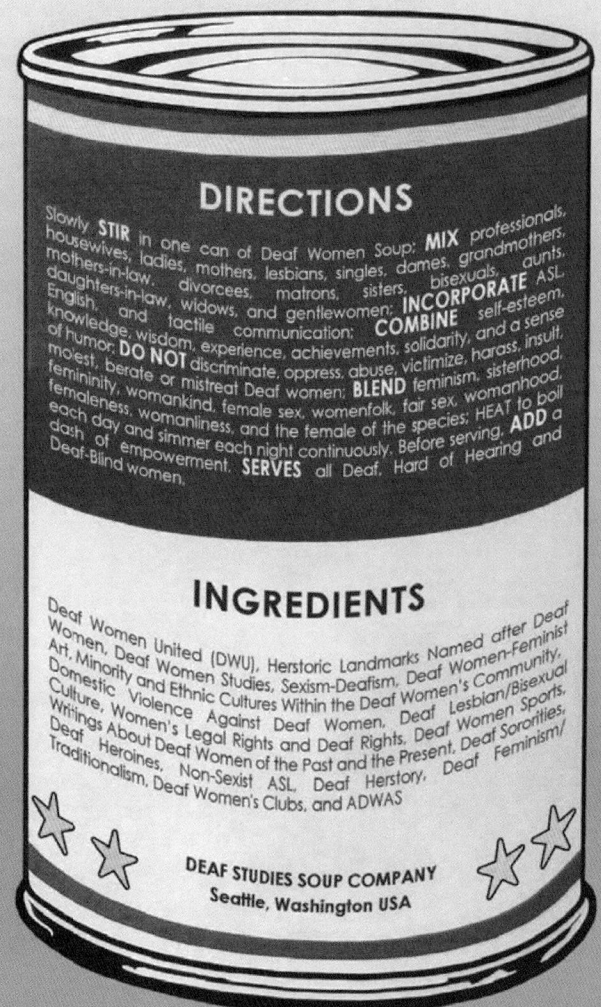

DIRECTIONS

Slowly **STIR** in one can of Deaf Women Soup; **MIX** professionals, housewives, ladies, mothers, lesbians, singles, dames, grandmothers, mothers-in-law, divorcees, matrons, sisters, bisexuals, aunts, daughters-in-law, widows, and gentlewomen; **INCORPORATE** ASL, English, and tactile communication; **COMBINE** self-esteem, knowledge, wisdom, experience, achievements, solidarity, and a sense of humor; **DO NOT** discriminate, oppress, abuse, victimize, harass, insult, molest, berate or mistreat Deaf women; **BLEND** feminism, sisterhood, femininity, womankind, female sex, womenfolk, fair sex, womanhood, femaleness, womanliness, and the female of the species; HEAT to boil each day and simmer each night continuously. Before serving, **ADD** a dash of empowerment. **SERVES** all Deaf, Hard of Hearing and Deaf-Blind women.

INGREDIENTS

Deaf Women United (DWU), Herstoric Landmarks Named after Deaf Women, Deaf Women Studies, Sexism-Deafism, Deaf Women-Feminist Art, Minority and Ethnic Cultures Within the Deaf Women's Community, Domestic Violence Against Deaf Women, Deaf Lesbian/Bisexual Culture, Women's Legal Rights and Deaf Rights, Deaf Women Sports, Writings About Deaf Women of the Past and the Present, Deaf Sororities, Deaf Heroines, Non-Sexist ASL, Deaf Herstory, Deaf Feminism/ Traditionalism, Deaf Women's Clubs, and ADWAS

DEAF STUDIES SOUP COMPANY
Seattle, Washington USA

▲ DEAF WOMEN SOUP | 1995
20" x 16" (50.8 x 40.6 cm)
2-D layered paper collage
Collection, Gallaudet University

DEAF STUDIES FOR RENT

1/5

Silver '92

DEAF STUDIES FOR RENT | 1992 ▲
20" x 16" (50.8 x 40.6 cm)
2-D layered paper collage
Private collection, New Jersey

ASLTA SOUP CANS | 1999 ▶
16" x 20" (40.6 x 50.8 cm)
2-D layered paper collage
Private collection, South Carolina

112

Chapter 10
YOU'VE GOT MAIL ART

BETWEEN THE SHADOWS CAST BY TWO dark buildings against a gray sky, a shadowy man stands with his arms crossed. The viewer can't see his mouth or eyes and his forearms are tied in two places. There is no way he could use ASL in this predicament.

Yet the caption reads **FREEDOM TO SPEAK OUT IN ASL**. The first words compete for attention among several stamps that each say "Is the Freedom to Speak Out a Root of Democracy?" With words unspoken, the arm-gagged man gives his answer...

The piece alludes to the long oppression of the language of Deaf people in most of North America: ASL. Because of its powerful message, the piece has had a productive life. This is the fourth book that has been graced with its presence.

▲ I + L + Y = LOVE STAMP | 1996
1" x 1.5" (2.5 x 3.8 cm)
ink on paper
Artist's collection, Seattle

FREEDOM TO SPEAK OUT IN ASL, No. 2 | 2012 ▲
11" x 17" (27.9 x 43.2 cm)
enlarged from 1993 Mail Art made with graphite and ink on envelope
with digitized stamps (2012)
Private collection, Chicago

KEN ROTHSCHILD • 41 OTHERLOOK DRIVE • SLOATSBURG, NY 10944

▲ DEAF STAMPS | 1997
9.5" x 4.1" (24.1 x 10.4 cm)
colored pencil and ink on envelope
with digitized stamps (2012)
Artist's collection, Seattle

RECOGNIZING KANNY | 1992 ▼
9.5" x 4.1" (24.1 x 10.4 cm)
colored pencil and ink on envelope
with digitized stamp (2012)
Artist's collection, Seattle

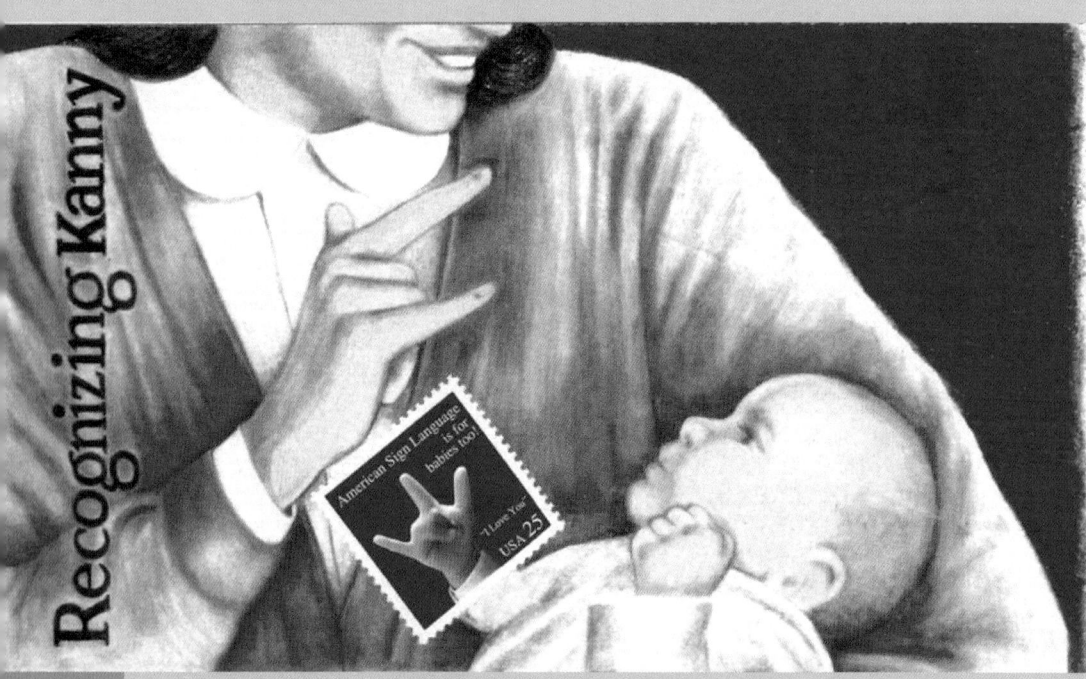

BARBARA
KANNAPELL

2522
RANDALL
AVENUE NE

WASHINGTON
DC 20017

M.J. Bienvenu · 2078 Jest Avenue · Chesterly, Maryland 20610

▲ DEAF RIGHTS | 1991
9.5" x 4.1" (24.1 x 10.4 cm)
colored pencil and ink on envelope
with digitized stamps (2012)
Artist's collection, Seattle

THE VOYAGE OF CLERC & GALLAUDET | 1993 ▼
9.5" x 4.1" (24.1 x 10.4 cm)
colored pencil and ink on envelope
with digitized stamp (2012)
Artist's collection, Seattle

▲ WORLD GAMES FOR THE DEAF | 1995
9.5" x 4.1" (24.1 x 10.4 cm)
colored pencil and ink on envelope
with digitized stamp (2012)
Artist's collection, Seattle

THOMAS H. GALLAUDET STAMP | 1989 ▼
9.5" x 4.1" (24.1 x 10.4 cm)
colored pencil and ink on envelope
with digitized stamps (2012)
Artist's collection, Seattle

▲ SIXTY YEARS OF SSDI | 1996
9.5" x 4.1" (24.1 x 10.4 cm)
colored pencil and ink on envelope
with digitized stamps (2012)
Artist's collection, Seattle

DEAF ART | 1986 ▼
9.5" x 4.1" (24.1 x 10.4 cm)
colored pencil and ink on envelope
with digitized stamp (2012)
Artist's collection, Seattle

▲ WASHINGTON ASLTA | 1992
9.5" x 4.1" (24.1 x 10.4 cm)
colored pencil and ink on envelope
with digitized stamps (2012)
Artist's collection, Seattle

ADWAS | 2004 ▼
9.5" x 4.1" (24.1 x 10.4 cm)
colored pencil and ink on envelope
with digitized stamps (2012)
Artist's collection, Seattle

1625 ΡΔΓΚ ΓΔΝΣ   ΚΣΓΜΔΝ, ΜΕ Φ4Φ43

▲ DEAF LESBIAN FESTIVAL (DLF) | 1999
9.5" x 4.1" (24.1 x 10.4 cm)
colored pencil and ink on envelope
with digitized stamps (2012)
Artist's collection, Seattle

I + L + Y = LOVE STAMP – first day cover | 1993 ▼
6.5" x 4.8" (16.5 x 12 cm)
ink on envelope
Artist's collection, Seattle

Chapter 11
ROAD SIGNS

CULTURAL - LINGUISTIC CROSSING, BI-BI | 1992 ▲
16" x 20" (40.6 x 50.8 cm)
2-D layered paper collage
Private collection, Connecticut

IN JUNE OF 1991, SILVER MOVED BACK TO Seattle to be closer to her mother. She had not yet unpacked and had boxes everywhere, but she wanted to surprise her friend MJ Bienvenu with a Deaftoon MJ could use in an upcoming edition of *TBC News,* a monthly newsletter.

Silver moved some boxes and crates to make a temporary desk, found some paper and a pen, and proceeded to create this Deaftoon depicting a police officer leaning against a sign: *DEAF CHILDREN AREA, NO COCHLEAR IMPLANTING BEYOND THIS POINT.* This started her thinking about many issues she wished were on road signs that pertained to Deaf people and Deaf culture. The most prolific period of artwork in her life started that night, the night she created her first road sign.

▲ COP ON SIGN : DEAF CHILDREN AREA,
NO COCHLEAR IMPLANTING | 1991
14" x 11" (35.6 x 27.9 cm)
ink drawing on paper
Artist's collection, Seattle

4-WAY STOP

LATE-DEAFENED WAY

HARD-OF-HEARING WAY

DEAF-BLIND WAY

ONE WAY

DEAF WAY

DEAF WAY

1/5

Silver '02

▲ 4-WAY STOP | 2002
16" x 20" (40.6 x 50.8 cm)
2-D layered paper collage
Private collection, Arizona

WE ARE
HAVING
TECHNICAL
DIFFICULTIES.

PLEASE
STAND BY.

WE ARE
HAVING
COMMUNICATION
DIFFICULTIES.

PLEASE
SUFFER.

COMMUNICATION
BREAKDOWN
AHEAD
2 min.

▲ TECHNICAL VS. COMMUNICATION
DIFFICULTIES | 1992
20" x 16" (50.8 x 40.6 cm)
2-D layered paper collage
Private collection, Georgia

◀ COMMUNICATION BREAKDOWN
AHEAD / 2 min. | 1992
16" x 20" (40.6 x 50.8 cm)
2-D layered paper collage
Private collection, New York

GA to SK?

When Silver created these pieces in 1992, the use of TTYs was going strong. Some who read this may not remember that the Deaf community once used TTYs to communicate. The WWII and Korean War surplus teletype machines were converted with a *Weitbrecht* modem to allow Deaf people to communicate with each other over the telephone. By 1990 it was common for Deaf people to have much newer and smaller machines that performed the same function, but took up much less space. Many public telephones were equipped with a pull out TTY in larger cities. Along with the machines from WWII came some terms for

Part of a series found later in this chapter, this pair of white signs, one with red lettering and one with green lettering, highlight terms for a TTY that the Deaf community never approved: TT, T, and TDD were bad choices. Regardless of the age or size of the machine, it was a TTY.

A *model 28 Teletypewriter typically converted and used as a TTY by many Deaf households in the early days of TTY communication.*

▼ TT, T & TDD : WRONG WAY /
TTY : RIGHT WAY │1992
20" x 16" (50.8 x 40.6 cm)
2-D layered paper collage
Artist's collection, Seattle

▲ GA / SK | 1992
20" x 16" (50.8 x 40.6 cm)
2-D layered paper collage
Private collection, Seattle

their use. *GA* was to signify that the other person could "Go Ahead" and type. The term *SK* stood for "Stop Keying," meaning the conversation was over, but many in the Deaf community still believe it meant "Send Kisses."

A *more modern style TTY used during the 1990s. While most Deaf people have switched to the use of videophones and video relay services, Silver still uses her TTY.*

The above piece is made up of two white signs with black outlines on weathered posts against a dark blue background. *GA* and two arrows, one pointing left, and one pointing right grace the first sign, in the second there is a bold *SK* and a red stop sign.

127

ONE WAY / DEAF WAY | 1992 ▶
16" x 20" (40.6 x 50.8 cm)
2-D layered paper collage
Artist's collection, Seattle

ONE WAY / DEAF WAY | 1996 ▲
20" x 16" (50.8 x 40.6 cm)
2-D layered paper collage
Collection, Gallaudet University

▲ ONE WAY / DEAF WAY | 2012
20" x 16" (50.8 x 40.6 cm)
2-D digital paper collage
Private collection, Chicago

ROAD SIGNS

William C. Stokoe, Jr.

Dr. Stokoe majored in classic languages in college and was convinced by a former alumnus to work at Gallaudet. He knew no sign language when he came to Gallaudet

William C. Stokoe, Jr., 1989

to teach English.

When Dr. Stokoe arrived, he was taken with the sign language he saw on campus, though he was told that what he was seeing was not a language. He soon realized this was something important to research and decided to study the language he was seeing.

While he never became a fluent user of ASL, he worked with a few others to create a dictionary of what he called, *American Sign Language*. Dr. Stokoe named it this because he had

seen sign languages in other countries and knew that this version was also used in Canada so *American* was an appropriate term. When Silver arrived at Gallaudet in 1968, Dr. Stokoe was Silver's English teacher. She kept up a wonderful friendship with him, visiting him when she could from time to time.

In 1992, ASL had been named for only 27 years. There were no states that had ASL teacher certification and few colleges and universities accepted ASL for college credit. The concept of acceptance of classes in ASL to fulfill college language requirements was only starting to be discussed and few programs offered it for college credit. The words *American Sign Language* were rarely used as the title for classes, with many using the illegitimate term *sign language* instead.

This piece depicting the familiar curves of a bright blue and red interstate highway marker with white lettering and a hazy gray background was timely, if not before its time in 1992. It was a post stating the path ahead was often misunderstood. This was the road to full acceptance of ASL as a legitimate language for every purpose, including that of a first language for children. With all that is positive that has happened since it was named, this piece still speaks to the need to continue to travel down this road until it grows into a superhighway.

LEGITIMIZE ASL | 1992 ▲
16" x 20" (40.6 x 50.8 cm)
2-D layered paper collage
Private collection, Virginia

Mary Beth Miller and Silver, c. 1978

Mary Beth Miller

"*Legendary Deaf actress and comedienne Mary Beth Miller taught me the importance of humor in ASL and Deaf culture.*"

Silver has always loved a good joke. Always clever and to the point, in the piece she plays a joke on Deaf jokes.

DEAF JOKE SIGNPOST | 1992 ▶
16" x 20" (40.6 x 50.8 cm)
2-D layered paper collage
Private collection, Texas

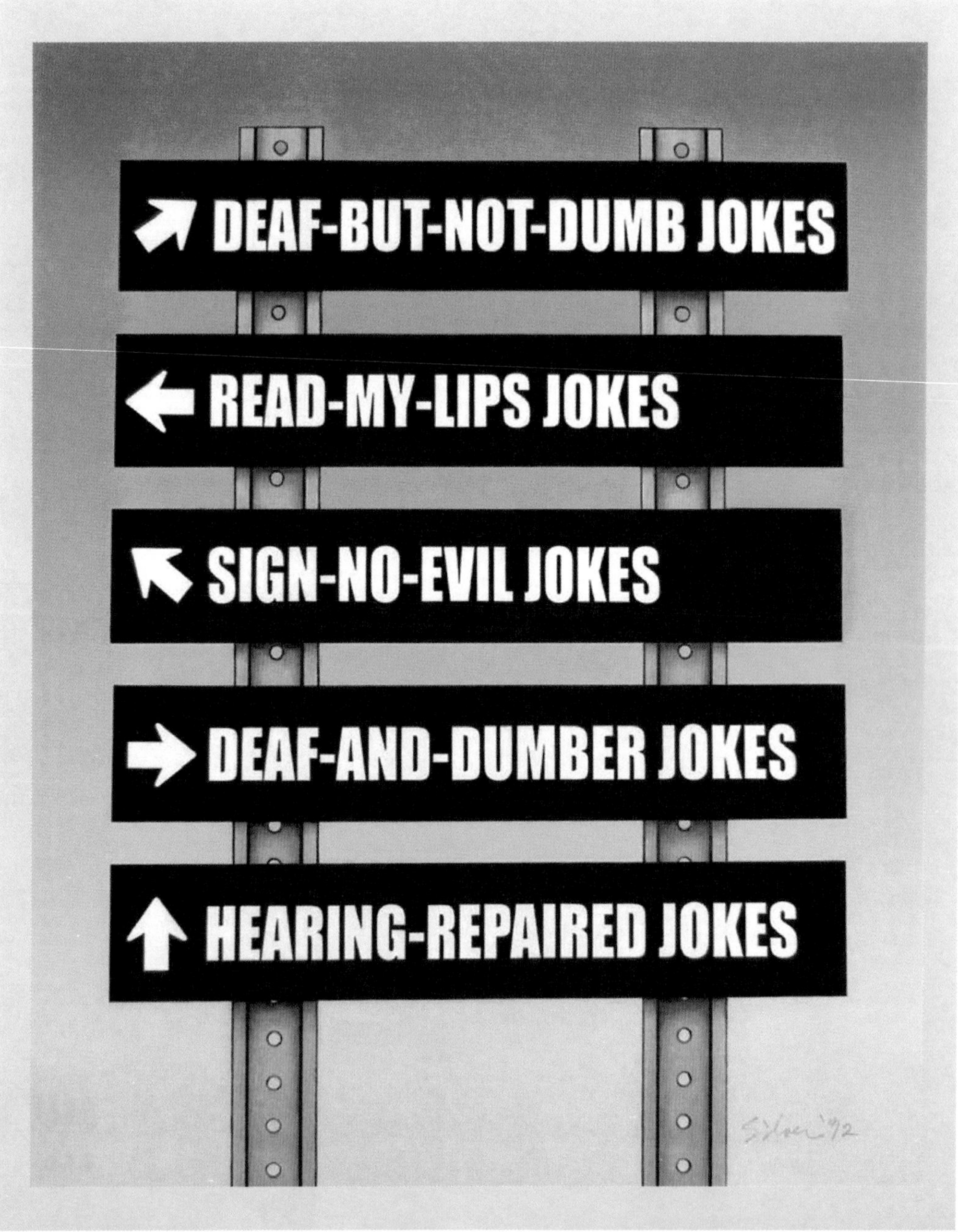

▲ DEAF HUMOR ONLY / ASL HUMOR ONLY | 1992
20" x 16" (50.8 x 40.6 cm)
2-D layered paper collage
Private collection, Delaware

ROAD SIGNS

DEAF IMPAIRED: WRONG WAY/ HEARING:
RIGHT WAY | 1992 ▶
20" x 16" (50.8 x 40.6 cm)
2-D layered paper collage
Artist's collection, Seattle

◀ HEARING IMPAIRED STUDIES: WRONG
WAY/ DEAF STUDIES: RIGHT WAY | 1992
20" x 16" (50.8 x 40.6 cm)
2-D layered paper collage
Artist's collection, Seattle

TT, T & TDD: WRONG WAY / TTY: RIGHT
WAY | 1992 ▶
20" x 16" (50.8 x 40.6 cm)
2-D layered paper collage
Artist's collection, Seattle

▲ HEARING IMPAIRED: WRONG WAY/ DEAF: RIGHT WAY | 1992
20" x 16" (50.8 x 40.6 cm)
2-D layered paper collage
Private collection, Indianapolis

"The words 'hearing-impaired' have a connotation of inferior social status. They promote an attitude of tragedy and imply powerlessness. Get this straight—as a woman, I am not penis-impaired. How long do you think schools would use that term to describe girls? They've been using the term 'hearing impaired' in schools since the early 1960s with no sign of stopping. Do they need a road sign to get this right? Here it is…"

MJ Bienvenu

Dr. Bienvenu comes from a Deaf family in Louisiana. She has been a staunch advocate of ASL and its use in every context possible. Countless students have seen her image on the cover of ASL books and she has been a force working from within the Deaf community for positive change. A long time friend of Silver's, Dr. Bienvenu has been a muse for a few of her pieces.

"I have to admit, I made this piece thinking of MJ. She is by far the fastest fingerspeller I have ever met. I think her fingers let off smoke sometimes from the friction of rubbing together. If the police enforced my road sign, she would get a speeding ticket every day."

MJ and Silver, 1992

FINGERSPELLING
SPEED LIMIT: 50
(red background) | 1992 ▶
16" x 20" (40.6 x 50.8 cm)
2-D layered paper collage
Private collection, Minnesota

▲ DEAF & DUMB, DEAF-MUTE: EXIT / DEAF: ENTER | 1992
20" x 16" (50.8 x 40.6 cm)
2-D layered paper collage
Private collection, New York

Notorious Deaf Labels

Some terms should have disappeared many years ago, yet they occasionally find their way into print and movies and are still used by thoughtless people from time to time. In this piece, Silver makes clear that the terms **DEAF & DUMB** and **DEAF-MUTE** can **EXIT** at the first opportunity and that the term **DEAF** should **ENTER** the minds of citizens when they want to discuss people of this cultural group.

Lou Fant

Lou Fant moved to the Seattle area two years before Silver moved back home from New York City. He was a versatile film, TV and stage actor who appeared in over 30 movies. He was also known as the Ace Hardware Man, the spokesperson for Ace Hardware from 1974 to 1980. They knew each other for many years and had much in common. Fant was a CODA (his parents were Deaf).

For his 60th surprise birthday party, those unable to attend were asked to send a video. Dressed in full geisha makeup and kimono, Silver signed a speech using Japanese Sign Language (JSL) and sent the top-secret video in for the party. The whole time she was in attendance at the party, Fant and others were trying to think of who he knew in Japan that could have sent that tape for the special occasion. No one recognized Silver until she came clean. His jaw-dropping moment was priceless.

Lou Fant, 1993

HEARING STUDIES /
DEAF STUDIES | 1992 ▶
16" x 20" (40.6 x 50.8 cm)
2-D layered paper collage
Artist's collection, Seattle

David Ludwig Bloch

David Ludwig Bloch was a Deaf woodcut artist and painter as well as a Jewish Holocaust survivor known for concentration camp-related Deaf art. In 1969, Silver's friend Simon J. Carmel drove her from Gallaudet to meet Bloch in Mt. Vernon NY. His Chinese wife Lilly, also Deaf, cooked a fantastic feast at which Silver and Bloch hit it off famously talking about art, history and culture.

When Silver lived in New York City, Bloch would frequently visit her on his weekly trips to the Union League of the Deaf in Times Square. They would attend interpreted Broadway shows or go to museums or antique shops together.

In 1987 Guy Wonder and Silver drove up to visit Bloch for lunch. He had all of his Holocaust-related artwork on display in his home to give them a sneak preview prior to moving it to a local museum for an exhibition. Wonder and Silver had splitting headaches on their return home after watching Bloch recount his first-hand experiences in the Dachau concentration camp.

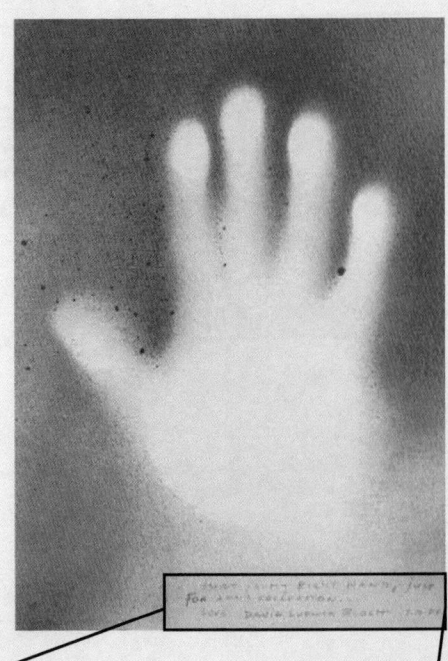

THAT IS MY RIGHT HAND — JUST FOR ANN'S COLLECTION. — LOVE DAVID LUDWIG BLOCH — 5.10.84

MY RIGHT HAND | 1984 ▲
David Ludwig Bloch
8" x 10" (20.3 x 25.4 cm)
blue spray-paint on paperboard
Artist's collection, Seattle

David Bloch, 1984

David Bloch looking at his artwork, 1984

"It was always funny to watch David mouth his words in German while he signed in ASL. It was almost like watching two languages at once."

▲ ASLTA AT WORK | 1992
16" x 20" (40.6 x 50.8 cm)
2-D layered paper collage
Private collection, Colorado

▲ ASL AT WORK | 1992
16" x 20" (40.6 x 50.8 cm)
2-D layered paper collage
Artist's collection, Seattle

DEAF STUDIES
AT WORK | 1992 ▶
16" x 20" (40.6 x 50.8 cm)
2-D layered paper collage
Artist's collection, Seattle

 DEAF LITERATURE /
 LITERATURE | 2002
16" x 20" (40.6 x 50.8 cm)
2-D layered paper collage
Private collection, Ohio

◀ DEAF LITERATURE /
ASL LITERATURE
(white sign) | 1992
16" x 20" (40.6 x 50.8 cm)
2-D layered paper collage
Artist's collection, Seattle

▲ DEAF LITERATURE /
ASL LITERATURE
(green sign) | 1992
16" x 20" (40.6 x 50.8 cm)
2-D layered paper collage
Private collection, Nebraska

141

Chapter 12

ARTISTIC ACTIVISM

FROM A YOUNG AGE, SILVER HAS ALWAYS seen and experienced injustice. Her mother modeled fighting injustice by writing letters to the editor of the *Seattle Times*, sending letters of complaint to various businesses, and rabble-rousing at city council hearings. Her example taught Silver to not sit back and accept the status quo.

Throughout high school and college she applied these lessons in her personal life, but when she returned to Seattle from New York in 1991, she let these ideas pour through her artwork to dramatic effect.

This chapter covers the important causes that reflect in her art including oppression, Deafism/Audism, cochlear implantation in children, the lack of focus on Deaf women's art, and Deaf gay pride.

▲ NO OPPRESSING
AT ANY TIME | 1992
16" x 20" (40.6 x 50.8 cm)
2-D layered paper collage
Artist's collection, Seattle

Pathologizing Deaf people is seeing them only as ears that don't hear that need repair and mouths that don't speak which need fixing. This is a recurring theme in Silver's work during the early 1990s. Much is lost when we marginalize and pigeonhole the people around us. Deaf people are much more than ears that don't function the same way as most and they seldom invest time thinking about their ears. With a deep blue sky in the background, this piece is designed like a warning sign. Silver uses red on white to emphasize that members of society *PATHOLOGIZE DEAF PEOPLE AT YOUR OWN RISK.*

▲ PATHOLOGIZE DEAF PEOPLE
AT YOUR OWN RISK | 1992
20" x 16" (50.8 x 40.6 cm)
2-D layered paper collage
Artist's collection, Seattle

A red triangular **YIELD** sign outlined in white with a blue sign gives the right of way to *Deaf Women*. A sister piece with the same **YIELD** sign but the smaller sign gives the right of way to *Deaf People*. Each of these is on a gray background, reminding one of fog. A Deaf person who isn't signing is as hard to identify as a road sign in the haze and it is appropriate to warn hearing people that the needs of Deaf people must be considered.

Silver has always been a fierce advocate for the Deaf rights. In these two pieces she reminds society that the needs of Deaf people and Deaf women should not be passed over.

YIELD TO DEAF WOMEN | 1992 ▲
16" x 20" (40.6 x 50.8 cm)
2-D layered paper collage
*Private collection,
Washington DC*

YIELD TO DEAF PEOPLE | 1992 ▶
16" x 20" (40.6 x 50.8 cm)
2-D layered paper collage
Private collection, Oregon

Deafism and Audism

Audism is a term coined in 1975 in Tom Humphries' Ph.D. dissertation. It means discrimination based on the lack of ability to hear. Silver coined the term *deafism* from the same time period and wrote several articles about *deafism* and *deafists* in *Silent News*. In some ways audism and deafism overlap, but deafism is a term that relates to discrimination that comes from the irrational fear of Deaf people and their culture and the cultural misunderstandings related to Deaf people. It is the predecessor of the term *surdophobia* coined by Gardy van Gils in 1997. Both terms relate to oppression of Deaf people that needs to end.

▲ WARNING: AUDISM IN PROGRESS | 1992
16" x 20" (40.6 x 50.8 cm)
2-D layered paper collage
Private collection, Oregon

◄ NO BLOCKING
SIGHTLINES | 1992
16" x 20" (40.6 x 50.8 cm)
2-D layered paper collage
Artist's collection, Seattle

▲ STOP DEAFISM | 1992
16" x 20" (40.6 x 50.8 cm)
2-D layered paper collage
Artist's collection, Seattle

The need for a clear line of sight between a Deaf person and the event they attend is something people frequently overlook. With wit Silver points this out with this NO PARKING sign parody.

145

▲ DEAF CHILDREN AREA / NO COCHLEAR
IMPLANTING BEYOND THIS POINT | 1992
16" x 20" (40.6 x 50.8 cm)
2-D layered paper collage
Artist's collection, Seattle

Implants in Small Children

A gray gradient background reminiscent of an overcast day is the backdrop for the diamond-shaped yellow and black sign stating this is a **DEAF CHILDREN AREA**, but this sign goes further and shares equal space with an additional marker beneath it on the same pole. This second sign is square and is black with a white border. It features a white silhouetted profile of a young boy. This cutout is similar to such silhouettes that were popular before photographs were possible in the early days of Deaf education from the mid-1700s through the early 1800s. This one, however, contains a modern warning, with the white on red **DO NOT ENTER** sign just behind the ear of the young boy. For those in the know, this message is clear: don't put cochlear implants into Deaf children. While feelings about such surgeries have been changing over the last 20 years, in 1992 it was a hot button issue and still remains a highly controversial topic in the Deaf community.

"I had these two pieces on display at a group show in association with the 1993 Deaf Studies III Conference in Chicago.

About halfway through the show, two registrants, both hearing women, came by looking at the various art on display. When they came to these pieces, they were so angry they actually took them off their easels! Because I happened to be close by, I ran up to them and told the women they had no right to censor my art or anyone else's and quickly set them right.

The women made such a fuss security had to be called and the women were asked to leave the exhibit area. I knew these pieces were controversial, but until that experience I had no idea how much emotion they might evoke."

▲ DEAF CHILDREN AREA : DO NOT ENTER | 1992
16" x 20" (40.6 x 50.8 cm)
2-D layered paper collage
Artist's collection, Seattle

147

Implants and Bottle Caps

With a white frame outline using a silver backdrop, this red and black piece looks familiar. A shiny red bottle cap sits center left in this piece, but has an odd cord coming out of the side that waves across the piece, separating the black from the red. On the red upper portion we see the start of something iconic and recognizable–the name of a well known thirst quencher. It soon becomes something odd— **Co-Chlear**. In the lower section in white letters, a play on a well-known phrase brings the message home— *IT'S NOT THE REAL THING*.

For the uninitiated, this says simply this: a cochlear implant is not real hearing. Regardless of advances in implant technology, the glamorous and hyped-up promotion cannot deny the fact that cochlear implants do not restore hearing to the level of a person who can hear and use spoken language. Silver's piece cuts the glamour in half and states the truth: it is artificial at best.

Co-Chlear | 1996 ▼
20" x 16" (50.8 x 40.6 cm)
2-D layered paper collage
Artist's collection, Seattle

This sister piece is more subtle in meaning. Using a bright green background, the red bottle cap becomes the sole focus of the piece this time, but it isn't a regular cap. There is an electric cord coming out of its side, snaking its way to something unseen. Is the big-ad bottle cap used to point out the huge cover-up of the truth about implants? No implant company posts success rates of their patients, but the Deaf community sees the many failed implant surgeries. Silver focuses attention on these aspects of **Co-Chlear** implants.

ARTISTIC ACTIVISM

*"My fellow distinguished ear surgeons,
you may wish to familiarize yourselves with this before
you begin drilling and wiring up Deaf babies."*

▲ A DEAF PRIMER | 1993
10" x 8" (25.4 x 20.3 cm)
Ink on paper
Artist's collection, Seattle

◄ DRIVE-THRU
COCHLEAR IMPLANT | 2002
8" x 10" (20.3 x 25.4 cm)
Ink on paper
Artist's collection, Seattle

GUILTY | 1996 ►
16" x 20" (40.6 x 50.8 cm)
2-D layered paper collage
Artist's collection, Seattle

INVENTOR & MANUFACTURER OF COCHLEAR IMPLANTS
GUILTY
FDA
GUILTY
PARENTS WITHOUT CONSCIENCE
GUILTY
EAR SURGEONS
GUILTY
SPEECH THERAPISTS & AUDIOLOGISTS
GUILTY
60 MINUTES
GUILTY
1/5
Silver '96

A Bilingual Question

The base of this piece is white lettering on a black background reminding one of the Vietnam War Memorial. In bright pink, red, and orange stands a question: **WHY NO DEAF WOMEN ARTISTS?** Silver made the question a bilingual one. The words **DEAF** and **WOMEN** are depicted in ASL fingerspelling with Caucasian flesh-colored hands, each containing a white-on-black boxed English letter corresponding to the fingerspelling on that hand.

This is yet another piece created during Silver's most prolific year. In this one, she points out that the little exposure Deaf Art received was mostly focused on the art of Deaf men. She lists nearly 100 women's names, and allows some of them to be obscured, making many who view the piece want to know the names behind the letters. Although many of these women are still living, some have stopped creating art. Their work is recognized in this piece—an ode to the Deaf woman artist.

Thanks, Mom

"My mother was always there for me, educating me not only artistically and personally, but also politically. My teachers also pushed me to think and view my work in various contexts. I would not be where I am today without them."

Belle and Silver, 1986

WHY NO DEAF WOMEN ARTISTS? | 1992 ▶
16" x 20" (40.6 x 50.8 cm)
2-D layered paper collage
Artist's collection, Seattle

PATHOLOGIZE DEAF PEOPLE AT YOUR OWN RISK

Chapter 12

ARTISTIC ACTIVISM

Guy Wonder and Silver, 2001

Guy Wonder

"Guy and I go a long way back. I still sport a scar he gave me in Coeur d'Alene, Idaho at a camp for deaf kids who used only speech and lipreading. He was very frustrated being around all the oralists. Guy's family was Deaf. He was the only person like that whom I knew.

Out of frustration from all the negative attitude from the oralists, he went off in a huff at one point and I followed him. He got to his cabin and slammed the screen door. Because he didn't realize I was that close behind him, without meaning to, he slammed it on my face. That left me a permanent below-the-lip scar by which to remember him.

I didn't know he was an artist until I saw him in Manhattan in the late 1960s. I would sometimes go to New York as a weekend escape while I was at Gallaudet. He loved having guests and I would stay at his spacious East Village loft.

Guy opened it up to Deaf folks who were visiting the city. He also let hearing artists stay there. He frequently had some from the Warhol Factory. All this was just around the time of the Stonewall Riots, when gays and lesbians protested against the way they had been treated at the Stonewall Inn in 1969. I went with Guy and other friends to the nation's

Bi-cultural sign?

The pink triangle was originally a Nazi concentration camp signifier for gay men. In the late 1970s it began its life as a symbol of gay pride; now it is a common identifier of the gay rights movement. Silver uses this icon and adds a white frame outline and white lettering in alternating English and ASL.

Silver is clever and expects people to bring something to the table to get the full experience from seeing her work. Due to this, and perhaps because the gay community has a much higher percentage of people who are bilingual, she chose not to interpret the ASL word **GAY** into English. To someone who can't fingerspell and doesn't know anything about the gay/lesbian/bisexual/transgender community, this sign means **DEAF & PROUD**- but to those in the know, it shows Deaf gay pride.

Silver at a gay pride parade, 2002

DEAF GAY & PROUD | 1992 ▶
16" x 20" (40.6 x 50.8 cm)
2-D layered paper collage
Private collection, New York

1/5　　　　　Silver '92

Guy Wonder (continued)

first gay pride parade in New York City (June 1970) while Los Angeles and Chicago also had theirs that summer.

Guy introduced me to many prominent people. He was my gateway to gay art culture, maybe **gayway** is a better word for it! We attended many parties together and many events as each other's date. He would come to DC often to visit. I can't remember the exact party the photo (below) was for, but we frequented the social scene in the NYC Deaf cultural arts community as well as New York Deaf Theatre and the visual and performing arts community. Guy was always there.

Silver (center) cross-dressed with two dates, 1975

Guy Wonder and Silver going to a party, 1969

We fought against hearing actors who would steal deaf roles. We also worked as outreach coordinators for the MoMA Educational Department by going to Deaf clubs and talking about the importance of going to museums with interpreting services. We did a lot together. During my time in New York, he was a fixture at private parties held in my home. Guy was my support system, for he was like a Deaf brother to me."

Need Relief?

This clever product is a parody of back relief cream. This time it is motivated by Silver's desire to end the oppression of the Deaf lesbi-gay-trans community. She does it here with a humorous, yet powerful political message.

▲ DEAF GAY CREAM | 1996
20" x 16" (50.8 x 40.6 cm)
2-D layered paper collage
Private collection, California

Chapter 13

25 THINGS

THERE ARE MANY THINGS ABOUT SILVER
with which you may not be familiar. Here
is a list of 25 things related to her artwork:

▲ I LOVE YOU LOVE STAMP | 1996
1" x 1.5" (2.5 x 3.8 cm)
ink on paper
Artist's collection, Seattle

1. Her favorite color is, you guessed it, silver.

2. Although she uses it to great effect, she does not care for the color orange.

3. Silver has five crates of more ideas for artwork.

4. David Bloch's piece, "Crying Hands," inspired her much-acclaimed ADWAS logo.

5. Mail Art is Silver's favorite type she has made.

6. Although she barely can operate a computer, she has a Facebook page for her fans.

❼ Silver had the idea for a non-ASL version of this piece (*Queerllogg's*) when she was still in high school.

▲ Queerllogg's | 1996
16" x 20" (40.6 x 50.8 cm)
2-D layered paper collage
Private collection, Georgia

Silver at work on the mural, 2001

▲ WASHINGTON SCHOOL
FOR THE DEAF | 2001
24' x 4' x 4 inches (7.3 x 1.2 m x 10.1 cm)
paint on cement with metal movement arrows
Washington School for the Deaf, Vancouver, WA

8 Silver created a large outdoor mural on the campus of the Washington School for the Deaf.

The mural on paper, 2001

9 She admits that, as a young kid, one of her earliest artistic influences was "Wacky Packages," a series of spoofed artwork that appeared regularly in MAD Magazine. The original artwork for each of the wacky packages now sells for six figures.

10 She once was drawing on a coffee table at a party and told legendary artist Keith Haring to stop smoking near her; he misunderstood her and thought she wanted him to get out so he left.

11 No art that she has made hangs on the walls of her home because she says it would clash with her Asian art and antiques.

The Silver tongue, 2001

▲ READ MY LIPS /
READ MY MIND
(peach) | 1992
16" x 20" (40.6 x 50.8 cm)
2-D layered paper collage
Artist's collection, Seattle

▲ FINGERSPELLING SPEED
LIMIT 50 (purple) | 1992
16" x 20" (40.6 x 50.8 cm)
2-D layered paper collage
Private collection, Chicago

12 She unconsciously sticks her tongue out whenever she concentrates on her art.

13 She has made alternate versions of several of her limited-edition pieces.

14 She keeps a pad of paper and a pen by her bed to write down art ideas she gets in the middle of the night and then sometimes can't read her own writing in the morning.

15 Her mother saved every piece of Mail Art Silver sent her for over 20 years. All of these pieces were destroyed by mold. *Please store your art collection in a clean, dry place!*

16 Other than Andy Warhol's soup cans, Susan Dupor (Deaf) and Paul Cadmus (hearing) are two of her favorite artists.

17 She once spent the entire day with artist LeRoy Neiman on Nov. 21, 1974 and he admitted to her that he had a hearing loss.

Silver and LeRoy Neiman
in the afternoon, 1974

LeRoy Neiman and Silver
in the evening, 1974

Silver's pre-Warhol
MOTORCYCLE, 1971

MONA LISA | 1962 ▶
8" x 10" (20.3 x 25.4 cm)
graphite on paper
Artist's collection, Seattle

18. The combined colors of light brown and olive green make her feel calm.

19. She made a copy of Mona Lisa and her "MOTORCYCLE" painting before Andy Warhol did.

20. She thinks she draws men better than she does women.

21. She would have loved to learn screenprinting, a technique she admires.

22. She has made commissioned artwork for friends.

23. She didn't sell her artwork until the mid-1990s when she was begged to do so by over 25 people. She didn't want to let her "babies" out into the world. When she realized she could make multiple versions of the same piece, she was willing to sell the "siblings."

CAST OUT | 1992 ▶
16" x 20" (40.6 x 50.8 cm)
2-D layered paper collage
Artist's collection, Seattle

▶ DEAF STUDIES
STATE MEANINGS.
DEAF ART
EXPRESSES THEM. | 1992
16" x 20" (40.6 x 50.8 cm)
2-D layered paper collage
Artist's collection, Seattle

▲ DEAF IS A VERB. | 1992
16" x 20" (40.6 x 50.8 cm)
2-D layered paper collage
Artist's collection, Seattle

DEAF ART COLORS
DEAF STUDIES. | 1992 ▶
16" x 20" (40.6 x 50.8 cm)
2-D layered paper collage
Artist's collection, Seattle

24 She made a series of
"Clipboard Art" pieces.

NOTE: As seen above in *DEAF ART COLORS
DEAF STUDIES*, the series includes artwork
highlighting her career-long crusade for
the inclusion of Deaf Art/ De'VIA in the
curriculum of Deaf Studies programs.

▲ IF IT ISN'T SIGN,
IT ISN'T LANGUAGE. | 1992
16" x 20" (40.6 x 50.8 cm)
2-D layered paper collage
Artist's collection, Seattle

25 Silver was recently honored by her inclusion in Tony Landon McGregor's two historic art pieces.

At the 2012 National Association of the Deaf (NAD) Conference and DeaFestival Kentucky in Louisville KY, Southwestern Deaf Art/ De'VIA artist Tony "Mac" Landon McGregor unveiled two pieces of art about the history of Deaf Art and Deaf artists. Both pieces contain prominently displayed images of Silver. In the smaller of the two pieces she is shown with her iconic piece, **HEARING IMPAIRED: WRONG WAY, DEAF: RIGHT WAY,** behind her as the second artist depicted between Betty G. Miller and Chuck Baird.

The artists depicted in order are:
Betty G. Miller,
Ann Silver,
Chuck Baird,
Sandi Inches Vasnick,
Susan Dupor,
Alex Wilhite,
Nancy Creighton,
Guy Wonder,
Shawn Richardson,
Mary Thornley,
Paul Johnston,
Joan Popovich-Kutscher,
Nancy Rourke,
Charles Wildbank,
Morris Broderson,
Jeff Carroll,
Paul Setzer,
William Sparks,
Harry R. Williams,
and
Tony Landon McGregor

20 AMERICAN-BORN DAM/De'VIA ARTISTS | 2012 ▲
Tony Landon McGregor, Ph.D.
16" x 20" (40.6 x 50.8 cm)
watercolor and ink on watercolor paper
Private collection, Seattle

▲ THE AMERICAN De'VIA ARTISTS FAMILY | 2012
Tony Landon McGregor, Ph.D.
60" x 36" (152 x 91 cm)
watercolor and ink on watercolor paper
Artist's collection, Texas

In this much larger second piece, McGregor places his image of Silver in the lower left-hand corner, holding a photograph of Harry R. Williams (HRW). Tony Mac's depiction of Brenda Schertz, the art curator, stands between Silver and his rendering of Betty G. Miller, seated on a Gallaudet throne. Miller's life partner, textile artist Nancy Creighton is shown next and ending the seated row is an image of Susan Dupor. Others depicted include Mary Thornley, Chuck Baird, Sandi Inches Vasnick, art historian and author Deborah Sonnenstrahl, Jeff Carroll, Tony "Mac" Landon McGregor, Paul Johnston, Alex Wilhite and Guy Wonder.

25 PERSONAL THINGS YOU PROBABLY DON'T KNOW ABOUT ANN SILVER

1. She fantasizes about becoming a tasting judge on "Iron Chef America."

2. She challenges anyone to a game of Scrabble or Pictionary.

3. She owns a collection of over 10,000 hands of all sizes and shapes.

4. She cannot tolerate oppressive summer heat and humidity.

5. She was the first Deaf signer to appear on "Antiques Roadshow," displaying an album of 300 autographs.

6. She is a faithful daily New York Times reader/TV news junkie.

7. She was a member of the feminist group, The Furies (1971-1972).

8. A dictionary is her all-time favorite book.

9. She loves to hang out in bookshops.

10. She once taught a chimp some ASL.

11. She is a lifelong flea market addict.

12. Her first spoken word was "thumb" – her second "vermouth."

13. She lives in Seattle and never drinks coffee.

14. She admires people who take care of the elderly.

15. She is not afraid of snakes.

16. She has stumpy thumbs that proudly run in the family.

17. She was trained in theatre design at the National Theatre of the Deaf Professional School.

18. She would like to be reincarnated as a cat, lazy and aloof.

Silver teaching a chimp how to sign, 1985

Silver needs a photostat ASAP, 1987

Photo by Steve Silver

19   She is a breast cancer survivor (since 2000).

20   She has been immortalized by a tile bearing her name in Pike Place Market, Seattle.

21   Favorite foods she rarely eats include dim sum, tater tots, latkes, petit-fours, root beer floats, and limeade.

22   She did a cameo in the MGM film, **Voices.**

Silver wrestles a python, 1992

23   She suffers from dyscalculia which explains why she is terrible at math.

24   She goes insane if a week goes by without sushi and admires things Japanese: antiques, ikebana, cuisine, tea gardens, art, bonsai, bamboo craft and traditional architecture.

25   Her favorite number is 25.

Silver points at her tile, c. 1988

An Asian sample of Silver's hand collection, 2012

Photo by Steve Silver

Silver in a wacky moment, 2004

Chapter 14
SILVER MOON BRAND

IT IS INTERESTING WHAT CAN COME FROM A friendship between two people. Silver was feeling several goals on her bucket list might never be accomplished before she met me. While she has good friends who look out for her, she hadn't been able to achieve what she wanted to with her artwork. Gallery art has been her only job since the early 1990s. The term *starving artist* was not meant to apply to a late-career artist of her caliber. It wasn't the quality of her work that was the problem—it was the technology gap.

As I said in the Preface, Silver and I hit it off from the start. Over the first couple of months we knew each other, we spent several hours at biweekly meetings chatting about art and life. I began to get a picture of what a talented artist loses when, for whatever reason, technology slips out of their grasp. The further away one gets from newer methods of creating artwork or from modern communication technology, the harder the newer ways are to grasp. The learning curve is steep and

HEARING LOSS

DEAF GAIN

▲ HEARING LOSS / DEAF GAIN | 2012
SILVER MOON BRAND
14" x 11" (35.6 x 27.9 cm)
ink drawing on paper
Private collection, Seattle

This inaugural piece from Silver Moon Brand takes something traditionally from the realm of hearing people and turns it on its ear... Deaf Gain emphasizes the positive contributions of Deaf people to society.

Quoting Bauman and Murray from Deaf Studies Digital Journal 1, in 2009, "Deaf Gain is defined as a reframing of DEAF as a form of sensory and cognitive diversity that has the potential to contribute to the greater good of humanity."

169

the technology gap had become a ravine in Silver's life.

Silver is one of the greats in Deaf Art. I realized to be able to help her would be a greater contribution to art than using that time to make my own.

Her complete lack of computer knowledge was clearly hurting her and she was stuck in a smaller and smaller world without personal access to newer ways of communication. Silver had been told more than once that she would no longer be faxed or mailed applications to art venues, and only email or internet submissions would suffice. Several competitions for grants and juried art shows also only had on-line applications. Doors were slamming in her face and she was out of the loop and she knew it.

The woman who more than 40 years ago, along with a handful of others paved the way for all Deaf Art and Deaf artists, was left out in the cold– with the harsh wind of change making it more and more artistically lonely for Silver with each passing year. The number of people on her holiday card list was getting smaller and smaller– she never received the e-cards they might have wanted to send her. Many thought she had died. Until reading this book, there may be some readers who think the same.

One day I handed her my first generation iPad and told her to go to the library and play with it. Slowly and I mean that word as literally as one can

"A couple of years ago I went into my favorite print shop to make some copies of a document and the owner said, "I'll be right back. I'm just going to burn your documents onto a disk."

I literally screamed! It took him 20 minutes to calm me down and assure me he wouldn't be harming my paperwork. It finally dawned on me that I was frozen in time, digitally speaking."

Tasty Deaf Pizza...

Attempting to be inclusive of a more marginalized group of members of the Deaf community, this piece cleverly replaces braille for the ridges on a tile from a popular game. Using red and blue on the interior of each design makes this piece a clear parody of a well-known chain, but it is one with a message for Deaf and hearing people alike. Don't discount or leave out Deaf-Blind people from the mix. The large white dots use braille to spell out **DEAF** on the top design and **DEAF BLIND** on the lower design.

DEAFINO'S PIZZA / DEAF BLINDO'S PIZZA | 2012 ▶
SILVER MOON BRAND
16" x 20" (40.6 x 50.8 cm)
2-D digital paper collage
Private collection, Seattle

mean it—slowly, she learned a little about the digital world. One thing she thought previously was that she could easily catch up on all the technology if someone would teach her. When I explained that I started using graphics art software programs in 1991 and have had to keep up year after year with countless changes in programs, styles and approaches to the work, she realized it would not happen like she envisioned.

I took my computer and hooked it up to her TV and we discussed design, graphics and digital art. Both of us were surprised to learn that we were thinking along the same lines and started working together on *THE PERIODIC TABLE OF DEAF CULTURE*. My background as an administrator and teacher came in handy on this piece and we found a way to work together successfully. Using the skills that Silver never lost combined with my own abilities, we became a team.

Whenever Silver asks why there is a fly in the middle of the piece on TV, thinking it was a live bug, I have to again

Jim and Silver at her solo show in Chicago, 2012

explain that it is the computer cursor. Over the course of time we have learned how to work together. Our sensibilities run in the same direction, although hers is traditionally based in many ways. And to say she is a font snob is putting it mildly. I'm sure Silver puts up with more from me than I do from her, and we both hope the resulting art is worth it in the end.

The crowd at Silver's solo show in Chicago, 2012

Natural Elements

In 2002 Silver painstakingly made **THE ELEMENTS OF DEAF CULTURE: A Periodic Table**. It displays 101 boxes containing a variety of components that make up Deaf Culture. In the last ten years, much within our community has changed.

THE PERIODIC TABLE OF DEAF CULTURE (following the next page) is bigger and includes more elements in every way, reflecting the maturing nature of Deaf society. On a light tan background, the black-outlined boxes with colorful centers make a pattern unlike any other periodic table.

THE ELEMENTS OF DEAF CULTURE: A Periodic Table

17 **Df** Deaf	52 **Wo** Deaf-World										68 **Jn** Junior NAD	44 **Dr** Deaf Rights					
61 **Hh** Hard of Hearing	22 **Co** Deaf Community	28 **Dc** Deaf Culture	84 **Pa** PAH!						60 **Hd** Hands	76 **Md** Miss Deaf America	8 **Ta** ASLTA	56 **Ea** Equal Access					
19 **Db** Deaf-Blind	34 **Di** d/Deaf Identity	42 **Dp** Deaf Pride	85 **Pe** Peddlers of ABC Cards	15 **Cm** Communication Systems	5 **Al** ASL Literacy	36 **Dt** Deafitecture	97 **St** ASL/Deaf Storytelling	32 **Hw** Deaf Hollywood	75 **Mr** Mirrors	45 **Sp** Deaf Sports	41 **Do** Deaf Organizations	99 **Ua** Universal Access					
69 **Ld** Late Deafened	49 **Vn** Deaf Values & Norms	31 **Dh** Deaf Heritage	3 **Sl** American Sign Language	59 **Go** Gestuno	4 **Lg** Linguistics	33 **Hs** Deaf Humor & Signlore	91 **Th** Signed Theatre	37 **Dj** Deaf Jokes	71 **Lh** Lighting	54 **Pz** DPN	39 **Dl** Deaf Life	10 **Au** Audism					
14 **Cd** CODA	20 **Cp** Deafcentric Paradigms	38 **Le** Deaf Legends	72 **Ma** Manual Alphabet	92 **Ch** Signing Chimps	101 **Vo** Voice-off	7 **Po** ASL Poetry	80 **Td** National Theatre of the Deaf	30 **Dg** Deaf Goodbyes	26 **Dy** Deaf-Friendly	51 **Wm** Deaf Women	78 **Nm** NADmag	35 **Dm** Deatism					
62 **Hg** Hearing	27 **Ft** The D-Factor Theory	70 **Lc** LeClerc	57 **Fs** Fingerspelling	67 **In** Interpreting	18 **Da** Deaf Art	6 **Li** ASL Literature	73 **Mi** Mime	66 **Ls** I-Love-You Sign	93 **Si** Silence	29 **Gl** Deaf GLBT	94 **Sn** Silent News	53 **Dn** Discrimination					
28 **Ge** Deaf Genetics	24 **Dv** Deaf Diversity	74 **Mt** The Milan Terror of 1880	79 **Ns** Name Signs	11 **Bi** Bi-Bi	48 **To** Deaftoons	40 **Lt** Deaf Literature	47 **Tf** Deaf TV/Film	50 **Dw** Deaf Way	21 **Cl** Deaf Clubs	77 **Nd** NAD	43 **Pu** Deaf Publications	83 **Op** Oppression					

13 **Cc** Closed Captioning	12 **Cf** Captioned Films/Videos	87 **Rs** Relay Services	100 **Vi** Video Relay	98 **Te** Tele-communications	9 **Ad** Assistive Devices	90 **Pr** Support Services Providers	81 **No** Note-takers	89 **Sa** Service Dogs	1 **Ac** Accessibility	63 **Ha** Hearing Aids	64 **Ba** Hearing-Aid Batteries
96 **Sc** State Commissions for the Deaf	86 **Ra** Rehabilitation Act	55 **Vr** Vocational Rehabilitation	2 **Dz** ADA	65 **Id** IDEA	95 **Ss** SSDI	25 **De** Deaf Education	88 **Sd** Schools for the Deaf	82 **Nt** NTID	16 **Cs** CSUN	58 **Gu** Gallaudet University	46 **Ds** Deaf Studies

▲ THE ELEMENTS OF DEAF CULTURE: A Periodic Table | 2002
20" x 16" (50.8 x 40.6 cm)
2-D layered paper collage
Collection, Gallaudet University, Washington DC

(next page)
THE PERIODIC TABLE OF DEAF CULTURE | 2012 ▶
SILVER MOON BRAND
20" x 16" (50.8 x 40.6 cm)
2-D digital collage
Private collection, France

76 **NAD** National Association of the Deaf	51 **VP** Videophone	36 **Da** Deaf Art/De'VIA				

Legend:
- PEOPLE
- CORE
- WAY OF LIFE
- LANGUAGE
- HISTORY
- VISUAL & PERFORMING ARTS

| 78 **Jn** Jr. NAD | 52 **Ft** FaceTime | 37 **Dm** Deaf Film/TV | 20 **Fs** Fingerspelling | | | |

| 80 **Nc** National Centers for Law & the Deaf | 53 **Vl** Deaf Vlogs/Blogs | 38 **NTD** National Theatre of the Deaf | 22 **Lg** ASL Linguistics | 6 **ASL** American Sign Language | 7 **Di** Deaf Identity | 1 **D** Deaf |

| 82 **DSA** Deaf Seniors of America | 54 **Rt** Real Time Captioning | 39 **Ha** Deaf Humor Deaf Jokes | 24 **Li** ASL Literature | 13 **De** Deaf Eyes | 10 **Wo** Deaf World | 3 **Hh** Hard of Hearing |

| 84 **Ad** American Association of the Deaf-Blind | 55 **Em** email | 56 **Tx** Texting | 40 **Tn** Deaftoons | 26 **As** ASL Storytelling | 15 **By** Deaf Goodbyes | 12 **Dg** Deaf Gain |

| 99 **Sc** State Offices & Commissions for the Deaf | 86 **Df** Deafhood Foundation | 87 **RAD** Rainbow Alliance of the Deaf | 58 **Cc** Closed Captioning | 41 **Df** Deaf Folklore | 28 **Bs** Baby Signs | 17 **Sp** Deaf Sports |

| 105 **Dn** Discrimination | 100 **ADA** Americans with Disabilities Act | 90 **Dv** ADWAS & DV Coalition | 67 **In** Interpreters | 60 **Tt** TTY | 42 **Mi** Mime | 19 **Dt** Deafitecture |

| 106 **Au** Audism | 107 **Sm** Deafism | 101 **Ra** Rehabilitation Act | 93 **Ch** American Society for Deaf Children | 69 **Vi** Video Interpreters | 62 **He** Hearing Aids | 63 **Vb** Vibrating Alarms |

| 108 **Or** Oralism | 109 **AGB** Alexander Graham Bell Association | 110 **Du** Deaf Eugenics | 103 **Id** Individuals with Disabilities Education Act | 96 **Ar** American Deafness & Rehabilitation Association | 71 **SSP** Support Service Providers | 72 **Ct** CART Providers |

| 111 **Ib** Cochlear Implants in Babies | 112 **Dɘd** Deaf Education | 113 **Hi** Hearing Impaired | 114 **Dd** Deaf & Dumb | 115 **Dx** Deaf Mute | 116 **Dy** Dummy | 117 **Dz** Deaf Exclusion & Marginalization |

BLE OF DEAF CULTURE

Legend:
- ☐ EDUCATION
- ☐ COMMUNICATION
- ☐ SERVICES
- ☐ ORGANIZATIONS
- ☐ GOVERNMENT
- ☐ BARRIERS

					43 Gu — Gallaudet University	**77** Cl — Deaf Clubs & Deaf Community Centers
			21 Ta — Tactile ASL	**30** Dh — Deaf History	**44** Nt — NTID	**79** RID — Registry of Interpreters for the Deaf
2 Db — Deaf-Blind	**8** Dp — Deaf Pride	**9** Dv — Deaf Values & Norms	**23** Al — ASL Literacy	**31** Su — Deaf CEOs & Superintendents	**45** Cs — CSUN	**81** WFD — World Federation of the Deaf
4 Ld — Late Deafened	**11** Dh — Deafhood	**14** Hs — Hands	**25** Po — ASL Poetry	**32** DPN — Deaf President Now Movement	**46** Sd — Schools for the Deaf	**83** At — ASL Teachers Association
5 Cd — Coda	**16** Pah — Pah!	**27** Ge — Gesture	**33** Dw — Deaf Way	**47** Dc — Deafcentric Education	**57** Ci — Cochlear Implants	**85** CIT — Conference of Interpreter Trainers
18 ILY — I-Love-You Sign	**29** Ns — Name Signs	**34** Dw² — Deaf Way II	**48** Ds — Deaf Studies Programs	**59** Ld — Assistive Listening Devices	**88** DWU — Deaf Women United	**89** Hd — National Council of Hispano Deaf & Hard of Hearing
35 Ut — Unity for Gallaudet Movement	**49** It — Interpreter Education	**50** Pu — Deaf Publications	**61** Cf — Captioned Films	**68** VRS — Video Relay Services	**91** BDA — National Black Deaf Advocates	**92** DAC — National Asian Deaf Congress
64 Va — Flashing Lights Visual Alarms	**65** Mr — Mirrors	**66** Pp — Pen & Paper	**70** Cdi — Deaf Interpreters	**94** TDI — Telecommunications for the Deaf, Inc.	**95** JDC — Jewish Deaf Congress	**102** Vr — Vocational Rehabilitation Services
73 No — Note Takers	**74** VCO — Voice Carry Over	**75** Sa — Service Animals	**97** St — USA Deaf Sports Federation	**98** Do — Deaflympics	**104** Ss — Social Security Disability Income (SSDI)	**2012 ©** SMB — Silver Moon Brand

8/100   Silver 錶   Jin Van Mann 月 2012

Chapter 14
SILVER MOON BRAND

The Solo Show

An historic event in the Deaf Art world took place in downtown Chicago. April 2, 2012 marked the opening night of Silver's first solo show which was held at Columbia College Chicago. Over 300 attended the reception that night and many more saw the 38-piece semi-retrospective.

Silver chats with visitors to the show, 2012

Some of the many who came to see the show, 2012

Crom Saunders and Peter Cook in a contemplative moment, 2012

> "In grade school I was confused about white and flesh-colored crayons to describe our skin.
>
> Like the makers of crayons at that time, I did not take into account the variety of flesh tones there are in society. I merely was stating the obvious as I saw it. 'I'm flesh, not white!' I protested. Crayon names shaped my consciousness of who we are as people.
>
> I continued my rebellion in high school. On forms I identified myself as 'flesh' in the 'Other' category."

DEAF DIVERSITY CRAYONS | 2012 ▶
SILVER MOON BRAND
16" x 20" (40.6 x 50.8 cm)
2-D digital collage
Private collection, Chicago

DEAF MULTI
DEAF LGBTQ AME
DEAF NATIVE A
DEAF ASIAN AMERIC
DEAF HISPANIC AME
DEAF AFRICAN AM
DEAF CAUCASIAN A
DEAF WOME
DEAF
DIVERSITY
crayons
colorize,
not
colonize

SILVER BIOGRAPHY

Born: May 25, 1949, Seattle WA

EDUCATION
1968 – Roosevelt High School, Seattle WA
1972 – Gallaudet University, Washington DC (BA, Art)
1977 – New York University, NYC NY (MA, Deaf-based Vocational Rehabilitation)

GRANTS & AWARDS
New York Governor's Arts Award (MoMA Programmatic Accessibility)
Joseph G. Blum Cultural Leadership Award
Japan-U.S. Friendship Commission Creative Fellowship
Outstanding Alumnus of the Year, Gallaudet University
Theatre Design Scholarship, National Theatre of the Deaf
National Arts Club Scholarship
West Coast Woman of the Year, Quota International
National ILY Sign Postage Stamp Design Competition Award
Numerous industry awards for logo and book cover designs

SOLO SHOWS
2012 – Ann Silver: ONE WAY, DEAF WAY–The Solo Show, Columbia College Chicago, Chicago IL

GROUP ART EXHIBITIONS
2012 – National Association of the Deaf Conference/DeaFest KY Art Exhibit, Louisville KY
2012 – Deaf Studies Today Conference Art Exhibit/Utah Valley University, Orem UT
2008 – Deaf Artists in the Community & Schools Art Exhibit, Dishman Art Museum, Beaumont TX
2008 – Deaf Artists in the Community & Schools Art Exhibit, Austin Children's Art Museum, Austin TX
2008 – Deaf Studies Today Conference Art Exhibit, Woodbury Art Museum, Orem UT
2008 – Deaf Art Night Exhibit, Seattle Public Library, Seattle WA
2004 – Images & Visions of a Culture Art Exhibit, aND Gallery, St. Paul MN
2002 – Deaf Way II International Arts Festival, Gallaudet University, Washington DC
2002 – Women of Wisdom 2002 Art Exhibit, Not Terminal Gallery, Seattle WA
2001 – Seeing through Deaf Eyes Art Exhibit, Prince Street Gallery & Blue Mountain Gallery, NYC NY
2001 – An Evening of Visual Arts Exhibit / Rainbow Alliance of the Deaf Conference, Seattle WA
2000 – First National Deaf Art Touring Exhibit (seven cities)
1999 – VSA Art & Soul International Visual Art Exhibition, Westin Bonaventure, Los Angeles CA
1999 – Visions through Deaf Eyes Art Exhibit, Central Intelligence Agency, Langley VA
1999 – Deaf Studies VI Conference Art Exhibit, Pro Arts Gallery, Oakland CA
1997 – Deaf Studies V Conference Art Exhibit, Gallaudet University, Washington DC
1996 – Second National ASL Literature Conference Art Exhibit, Switzer Gallery, Rochester NY
1995 – Deaf Women United Conference Art Exhibit, Seattle WA
1995 – ASLFestival '95 Art Show, Pomona CA
1994 – Deaf Studies IV Conference Art Show, Boston MA
1994 – ASL Festival '94 Art Show, Pomona CA
1994 – Employing Artistry Art Exhibit, Seattle Center, Seattle WA
1994 – Deaf Art Exhibit, Seattle Central Community College, Seattle WA
1993 – Deaf Art Exhibit, AT&T/US West TTY Relay Center, Seattle WA
1993 – Deaf Studies III Conference Art Exhibit, Chicago IL
1993 – Women's Caucus for Art NW Regional Exhibit, Seattle WA
1989 – Deaf Way International Arts Festival, Gallaudet University, Washington DC
1985 – World Games for the Deaf International Arts Festival, Pepperdine University, Malibu CA
1985 – Artists with Disabilities Art Exhibit, Loeb Center Gallery/New York University, NYC NY
1983 – D.E.A.F. Media's Celebration '83, University of California at Berkeley

Silver, A., & Barwiolek, A. R. (Eds.).(1973). *The Red Barn '73.* Waterford, CT: National Theatre of the Deaf.

Silver, A. (1978). Letter to the editor: On the disability rights movement. *New York Post,* February 25.

Silver, A. (1980). MoMA initiates a program in ten NYC museums for deaf and hard of hearing museum visitors. *Silent News,* p. 9. February.

Silver, A. (1982). Interview with Dr. Betty G. Miller. New York, NY. On videotape (VHS).

Silver, A. (1983). Letter to the editor: Negative term. *New York Post,* February 3.

Silver, A. (1985). WGD art festival - the cultural impact of deaf artists. *Silent News,* pp. 24-25. November.

Silver. A. (1986). Letter to the editor: Censoring the deaf. *Asahi Evening News.* Tokyo, Japan. July 2.

Silver, A. (1989). Deaf Art and the manifesto. *Silent News,* pp. 7-8. September.

Silver, A. (1991). Letter to the editor: No small task. *TBC News 40*/October 1991, p. 4.

Silver, A. (1992). An open letter to Don Hewitt, executive producer of 60 Minutes: Cochlear implant: sure-fire prescription for long-term disaster. *TBC News 53*/December 1992, pp. 4-5.

Silver, A. (1992). Letter to the editor: The role and value of Deaf Art in deaf studies. *Gallaudet Alumni Newsletter,* vol. 27, no. 1, p. 6. September.

Silver, A. (1993). Why no deaf women artists? *TBC News,* July-August 1993.

Silver, A. (1993). School essay. In Eyes of Desire: *A Deaf Gay & Lesbian Reader,* edited by Luczak, R., pp. 18-19. Boston, MA: Alyson Publications, Inc.

Silver, A. (1993). Women, feminism and Deaf Art. In *Deaf Women United Conference Program Book, October 1993.* New Brunswick, NJ: Deaf Women United.

Silver, A. (1993). Reframing Deaf Art/De'VIA for the 21st century: New directions. In *Conference Proceedings of Deaf Studies III: Bridging Cultures in the 21st Century, Chicago IL, April 22-25, 1993,* pp. 67-74, edited by Cebe, J. Gallaudet University.

Silver, A. (1993). Questions about quality and purpose of deaf studies: The quest for academic legitimacy at Gallaudet University. *Art Scholar-in-Residence Critique,* May 1993. Olympia, WA: Washington State Arts Commission.

Silver, A. (1994). How does Hollywood see us, and how do we see Hollywood? In *The Deaf Way: Perspectives from the International Conference on Deaf Culture,* edited by Erting, C. J., Johnson, R. C., Smith, D. L., & Snider, B. D., pp. 731-735. Washington, DC: Gallaudet University Press.

Silver, A. (1994). Memories of Fred Schreiber. *The NAD Broadcaster,* p. 6. September.

Silver, A. (1996). Member visions and predictions for 1996. *The NAD Broadcaster,* pp. 1-2, vol. 18, no. 1. January.

Silver, A. (1997). Thou shall speak for, with, by and of. In *Who Speaks for the Deaf Community, A Deaf American Monograph,* vol. 47, pp. 53-55. Silver Spring, MD: National Association of the Deaf.

Silver, A. (2000). My experience as an artist vis-à-vis Deaf Art. In Sapir, J. D. (Ed.), *Visual Anthropology Review,* vol. 15, no. 2, pp. 37-46. Fall & Winter 1999-2000. Arlington, VA: American Anthropological Association.

Silver, A. (2009). Deaf Survivor: Ann Silver. In *Signs of Courage: Deaf Survivors of Breast Cancer, 3rd edition,* edited by Singleton, B., pp. 81-83. Surprise, AZ: Singleton Books.

An Interview with Ann Silver. *The Yomiuri Shimbun,* Tokyo, Japan. September 7, 1986.

Ann Silver and White Mare, Inc. *Media Report to Women,* July-August 1985.

Artists with Disabilities Art Exhibit Catalog, April 15-19, 1985. New York, NY: Loeb Center Gallery, New York University.

Bienvenu, M. J. (1993). Where is Ann Silver, the deaf artist? Plenary speech in *Conference Proceedings of Deaf Studies III: Bridging Cultures in the 21st Century, Chicago IL, April 22-25, 1993, pp. 7-18,* edited by Cebe, J. Gallaudet University.

Brandon, J. & Rinehart, D. B. (1994). *Employing Artistry: Art Exhibit Catalog, May 17, 1994.* Seattle, WA: Access '94.

Carroll, C. (Ed.).(1987). American in Japan: Ann Silver. *World Around You, pp. 1, 3, & 7-8.* February.

Celebrating 25 years - Notable alumni: Ann Silver, '72. *Gallaudet Today,* vol. 25, no. 4, p. 8. Summer 1995.

Class News & Notes: Ann Silver. *Gallaudet Today,* vol. 34, no. 1. Fall 2003.

Dalton, P. I. (1985). Ann Silver's sign language interpreting logo design. *Library Service to the Deaf and Hard of Hearing,* p. 344. Phoenix, AZ: The Oryx Press.

Deaf Artists: Ann Silver -- in *1994 Sign Language Videotape Collection Catalog,* pp. inside cover, 4, 12 & 24. Burtonsville, MD: Sign Media, Inc.

Dror, S. A. (1988). Ann Silver in *Deaf Trivia*, pp. 10, 12, 21 & 24. Los Angeles, CA: National Congress of Jewish Deaf, Inc.

Durr, P. (2000). Deconstructing the forced assimilation of deaf people via De'VIA resistance and affirmation art. In Sapir, J. D. (Ed.), *Visual Anthropology Review*, vol. 15, no. 2, pp. 47-68. Fall/Winter 1999-2000. Arlington, VA: American Anthropological Association.

Duval, W., Insana, L., Smutz, J., & Herlihy, Caitlin (Eds.). (1999). *Art & Soul International Visual Art Exhibition Catalog, May 29-31, 1999*. Washington, DC: VerySpecialArts.

Elion, L. K. (1999). My eyes are my ears. The art of Harry R. Williams. In *Conference Proceedings of Deaf Studies VI: Making the Connection, Oakland, CA, April 8-11, 1999*, pp. 37-44, edited by Cebe, J. Gallaudet University.

Erting, C. J., Johnson, R. C., Smith, D. L., & Snider, B. D. (Eds.).(1994). *The Deaf Way: Perspectives from the International Conference on Deaf Culture*. Washington, DC: Gallaudet University Press.

French, M. M. (1988). Ann Silver: A deaf safari to Japan. *Deaf Community News*, vol. 11, no. 1. January.

Gannon, J. R. (1989). *The Week the World Heard Gallaudet*. Washington, DC: Gallaudet University Press.

Gilbert, L-J. (1982). Access to the arts – New York's museums offer programs to the deaf community. *Gallaudet Today*, vol. 13, no. 1, pp. 23-27. Fall.

Gilbert, L-J. (1982). Meet Ann Silver – sign language designer/illustrator. *Gallaudet Today*, vol. 13, no. 1, pp. 1-5. Fall.

Goodstein, H., & Brown, L. (2004). *Deaf Way II: An International Celebration*. Washington, DC: Gallaudet University Press.

Greer, L. C., Holcomb, B. R., Long, D. D., Bancroft, C. F., Levitan, L., & White, D. (Eds.). (1999). *Celebrating sign language through the arts catalog for the National ASLTA Conference, October 8, 1999*. Rochester, NY: MSM Productions, Ltd.

Hammontree, M. (1998). Sounding off: a hearing woman checks out the deaf gay community. *Baltimore Alternative*, pp. 15-17. January.

Holcomb, M., & Wood, S. K. (1989). Art: Ann Silver. *Deaf Women: A Parade Through the Decades*, pp. 40-41. Berkeley, CA: DawnSignPress.

Holcomb, T. K. (2012). *Introduction to American Deaf Culture*. New York, NY: Oxford University Press, Inc. (in press).

How to draw a crowd of one million people. *The Japan Times*. May 18, 1986.

Huynh, A. (2012). Deaf culture represented at film festival. *The Daily (of the University of Washington)*, vol. 136, issue 6, p. 5. April 2.

Jacobowitz, E. L. (1992). Humor and wit in the deaf community. In *Conference Proceedings of Deaf Studies: What's Up? Washington, DC, October 24-25, 1992*, pp. 187-195, edited by Cebe, J. Washington, DC: Gallaudet University.

Juarbe, N. (1984). Celebration of Deaf Art. *The NAD Broadcaster*, Vol. 6, No. 5. May.

Kennedy admirer: girl, 11, helps greet idol, watches his every move. *The Seattle Times*. September 7, 1960.

Kushner, L., & Alpert, J. (2001). *Seeing Through Deaf Eyes Art Exhibit Catalog, June 5-23, 2001*. New York, NY: Prince Street Gallery and Blue Mountain Gallery.

Lane, H. (2004). *A Deaf Artist in Early America: The Worlds of John Brewster Jr.*, pp. 123-124. Boston, MA: Beacon Press.

Lane, H., Hoffmeister, R., & Bahan, B. (1996). *A Journey into the DEAF-WORLD*, pp. 141-142 & 485. San Diego, CA: Dawn SignPress.

Levitan, L., Bancroft, C. F., & Greer, L. C. (Eds.). (2003). Celebrating sign language through the arts catalog for the *National ASLTA Conference, April 11, 2003*. Rochester, NY: MSM Productions, Ltd.

Mann, J. (Ed.).(1999). Art criticism & history: De'VIA contributions to deaf studies panel moderated by Johnston, P., in *Conference Proceedings of Deaf Studies VI: Making the Connection, Oakland, CA, April 8-11, 1999*, pp. 391-412, edited by Cebe, J. Washington, DC: College for Continuing Education, Gallaudet University.

Martinez, M. V. (Ed.).(1987). Renowned American artist travels through Japan. *International Perspective*, vol. 2, no. 1, p. 3. Washington, DC: International Center on Deafness, Gallaudet University. September.

McDanel, B. (2004). An interview with artist Ann Silver. *WSDAA Newsletter*, pp. 11-13. Winter.

Media Report to Women, July-August 1985.

Meyers, K., & Willenbring, J. (2004). *Images and Visions of a Culture – Art Exhibit Catalog*. St. Paul, MN: aND Gallery.

Minkin, M., & Kool, S. (Eds.).(1992). Congratulations to Ann Silver (national ILY sign stamp competition). *FECCD Newsletter*, p. 7. Fall.

Moore, M. S., & Levitan, L. (1989). Plenary presentations: Ann Silver. Deaf Life, October.

Moore, M. S., & Levitan, L. (2009). Deaf almanac: Ann Silver. *Deaf Life*. May.

Moore, M. S., & Levitan, L. (2012). Subverting the stereotypes: Ann Silver. 2012 *Deaf Life Calendar*. Rochester, NY: MSM Productions, Ltd.

Moore, N. (1989). Spotlighting talent among deaf people of the world. *Gallaudet Today*, pp. 11-13. Fall.

Moseley, V., & Hummel, J. (1994). *SCCC Art Show Catalog, June 23-26, 1994*. Seattle, WA: Seattle Central Community College.

National Endowment for the Arts (1994). *Design for Accessibility – An Art Administrator's Guide*. Washington, DC: National Endowment for the Arts.

Nomeland, M. M., & Nomeland, R. E. (2012). *The Deaf Community in America: History in the Making*, p. 160. Jefferson, NC: McFarland & Company, Inc.

Polk, A., & Kaftan, C. (2002). Arts festival – Deaf way II 2002 special issue. *Gallaudet Today*, vol. 33, no. 1. Fall.

Rosenbaum, D. (1994). *ASL Festival '94 Art Show Catalog*. Pomona, CA: DeafExpo.

Rosenbaum, D. (2007). Where are they now: Ann Silver. *SIGNews,* vol. 5, issue 7, p. 17. July.

Roth, R. I. (Ed.).(2001). An evening of visual arts -- art exhibit catalog for the *Rainbow Alliance of the Deaf National Conference, July 5, 2001.* Seattle, WA: NWRAD.

Rothschild, K. (1993). NAD cachets available. *The NAD Broadcaster,* p. 31. October.

Rothschild, K. (1993). The new IL_Y stamp: Bypassing the deaf community. *Deaf Life,* page 36-39. April.

Schertz, B. (Ed.). (1995) *Deaf Artists' Exhibit Gallery Guide for the Deaf Studies IV Conference: Visions of the Past, Visions for the Future, Boston, MA, April 27-30, 1995.* Washington, DC: College for Continuing Education, Gallaudet University.

Schertz, B. (Ed.). (1997) *Deaf Artists' Exhibit Gallery Guide for the Deaf Studies V Conference: Toward 2000 – Unity & Diversity, Washington, DC, April 17-20, 1997.* Washington, DC: College for Continuing Education, Gallaudet University

Schertz, B. (1999). *Deaf Artist's Exhibit – Pro Arts Gallery Guide for the Deaf Studies VI Conference, April 8-11, 1999.* Washington, DC: College for Continuing Education, Gallaudet University.

Schertz, B. (1999). 20 deaf artists: Common motifs – deaf artists' exhibit at deaf studies VI conference. In *Conference Proceedings of Deaf Studies VI: Making the Connection, Oakland, CA, April 8-11, 1999,* pp. 417-439, edited by Cebe, J. Washington, DC: College for Continuing Education, Gallaudet University.

Schertz, B., & Lane, H. (2000). Elements of a culture: Visions by deaf artists. In Sapir, J. D. (Ed.), *Visual Anthropology Review,* vol. 15, no. 2, pp. 20-36. Fall & Winter 1999-2000. Arlington VA: American Anthropological Association.

Schertz, B. (2008). De'VIA Deaf Artist's Exhibit – "De'VIA: The Deaf Vernacular" at the Woodbury Museum. In *Deaf Studies Today! 2008 Montage, April 8-11, 2008.* Orem, UT: Utah Valley University.

Simpson, L. (1984). Profile: Ann Silver. *The Shadow Newsletter,* vol. 2, no. 1. Atlanta, GA: Stage Hands. Fall.

Smith, A. K., & Jacobowitz, E. L. (2005). *Have You Seen…? An American Sign Language (ASL) Handshape DVD/Book.* Frederick, MD: ASL Rose.

Smith, T. (1997). Deaf people in context. *Ph.D. dissertation,* University of Washington.

Sonnenstrahl, D. M. (1996). De'VIA: what an odd word! In Deafness: Historical Perspectives, A *Deaf American Monograph,* vol. 46, pp. 131-134. Silver Spring, MD: National Association of the Deaf.

Sonnenstrahl, D. M. (2002). *Deaf Artists in America: Colonial to Contemporary,* pp. 324-329. San Diego, CA: DawnSignPress.

Thornley, M. (Ed.). (2002). Ann Silver, USA. In *Deaf Way II Featured Visual Artists.* Washington, DC: Gallaudet University.

Van Manen, J. W. (2012). *Ann Silver: One Way, Deaf Way – The Solo Show Catalog.* Chicago, IL: Columbia College Chicago.

Walker, L. A., & Richner, N. R. (1983). *Museum Accessibility for Hearing-Impaired People, 1979-1983.* New York, NY: The Museum of Modern Art.

Willard, T. (1986). Ann Silver designs ASL greeting cards. *Deaf Artists of America Newsletter,* vol. 1, no. 1, p. 1. Winter.

Willard, T., & McKenney, S. (1996). *Second National ASL Literature Conference Art Exhibit Catalog, March 28-April 3, 1996.* Rochester, NY: Switzer Gallery, National Technical Institute for the Deaf.

Zinza, J. E. (2006). *Master ASL! Level One,* pp. 53, 68, 161 & 288. Burtonsville, MD: Sign Media, Inc.

Zinza, J. E. (2013). *Master ASL! Level Two.* Burtonsville, MD: Sign Media, Inc. (in press).

SILVER TELEVISION APPEARANCES

"Antiques Roadshow" (PBS) February 3, 2003

Deaf talk show (Deaf Mosaic, Gallaudet University) May 1986

Deaf talk show (NHK-TV, Japan) September 21, 1986 and September 28, 1986

Deaf talk show (Swedish Educational Broadcasting, Sweden) Summer, 1989

"Entertainment Tonight" (CBS) September 5, 1989

"World News Tonight with Peter Jennings" (ABC) May 9, 1979

INDEX OF ART

Artwork Title | Year   Page

INDEX OF ART

SILVER ACKNOWLEDGEMENTS

"During the 1970s, a significant community firestorm ended my promising career at Gallaudet, thanks to Fred Schreiber. Led by Fred and his NAD cohorts, the battle centered on the disturbing proliferation of sign systems invented by people in the name of Deaf Education. The latest target of the bitter controversy was the Signed English Project, a research unit I was involved with.

Having witnessed one of the epic pre-DPN events of the 20th century, my awakening to the existence of communication abuse, negative power and bastardization of ASL led to my resignation from Gallaudet. To get away from the oppressive climate of Kendall Green, I moved to New York City.

One day en route to work at New York University's Deafness Research & Training Center, I rode an elevator to my office. A floor later, in the elevator stepped Fred who was on his way to a board meeting. Seeing him triggered painful memories of the event many moons ago. Though I found his larger-than-life presence intimidating, my conscience urged me to thank Fred for setting the stage for what was to become my lifelong journey of Deaf community activism/advocacy.

When I mustered up enough courage to identify myself to Fred, the dilapidated elevator got trapped between floors. Oh great. The two of us stood awkwardly alone, exchanging nervous glances for what seemed like eternity. It took Fred a long time to maneuver the elevator controls until he succeeded in getting the cage to budge. The doors finally opened, much to our tremendous relief. Just as I was about to tap Fred's shoulder, he disappeared into the crowds – never to be seen again.

Having failed to personally thank Fred for the tremendous impact he had upon me, I carry that debt of gratitude inside me. Perhaps the lesson learned is to remember to acknowledge others and their contributions while we still have the breath to exchange greetings and embrace the ongoing struggle for Deaf rights as well."

—Ann Silver

("Memories of Fred Schreiber" reprinted from *The NAD Broadcaster*, September 1994)

"My appreciation to the following people who have influenced and helped me in my life who aren't already mentioned elsewhere:

Chuck Baird, Alan R. Barwiolek, the Myrna and Irwin Berch Family, the Mollie and Julian Berch Family, Jay Blumenfeld, Karen Bosley, Bernard Bragg, Judith and Phil Bravin, Dan Brubaker, Bill Burback, Simon J. Carmel, Joseph Castronovo, Barry Chernick, Nancy Silver Cochran, Columbia College Chicago, Peter Cook, Liza Cowan, Cliff Dehnhoff, Muriel Diamond, Susan Dupor, Lauren Fabella, Gallaudet University, Gertie Galloway, Eric Gangloff, Jack R. Gannon, Genie Gertz, Carole L. Glickfeld, Julius Goldstein, Bruce Hlibok, Eiichi and Satomi Honda, Brett Finley Iimura, Masao Itoh, Tetsuya Izaki, Jane Jacobs, Japan-U.S. Friendship Commission, Jewish Family Service, Paul Johnston, Jill Goodlatte Lensbower, Ella Mae Lentz, Faustino Lopez, Jackie Mann, Lewis Merkin, Matthew S. Moore, Donna Platt, Dorothy (Dot) Miles, Marlyn Minkin, National Endowment for the Arts, Yutaka Osugi, Claire Park, Perfect Copy & Print, Marie Philip, Mineko Ran, Robert I. Roth, Brenda Schertz, Vicki Shank, Steve Silver, Deborah M. Sonnenstrahl, Linda C. Stein, Martin L. A. Sternberg, Barb Tamura, Paula Terry, Martin Thompson, Mary Thornley, Michiko Morimoto Tsuchiya, Huberta W. Ugur, Gunilla Wagstrom-Lundqvist, Akihiro Yonaiyama, my unsung teachers, and my loyal fans and buyers of my artwork.

Last but most importantly, I am eternally indebted to Jim Van Manen. This book would not have been possible without him and he has given me a second act as an artist."

— Silver

James W. Van Manen was born in Sonoma CA, the second son to Deaf parents. He is a CODA (Child of Deaf Adults). His father graduated from the Iowa School for the Deaf, and his mother from the California School for the Deaf in Berkeley CA. He grew up in several states, including California, Wisconsin, Michigan, and Iowa.

Van Manen earned a BA in Teaching English to Speakers of Other Languages (TESOL) from the University of Northern Iowa in 1990. He earned his MA in Linguistics of Signed Languages from Gallaudet University in 1997 and completed his Ph.D. in Special Education Administration in 2007, also from Gallaudet University.

He has worked as a college professor in Chicago IL, Indianapolis IN, and Fremont, OH. He was the director of Deaf and Hard of Hearing Services in Indiana for eight years and has worked as an interpreter in Iowa, Ohio, Washington DC, Maryland, Virginia, Indiana, and Illinois.

Van Manen is an avid reader about art and artists. He has taken courses on digital graphics programs since 1990. In his spare time he worked as a wire sculptor from 1998 to 2003– sculpting hands. He started painting hands in acrylic in 2003. Wire sculptures, painting and digital art have been based on his experiences growing up in a Deaf home.

Van Manen has loved Pop Art since he first saw it in the 1970s. Keith Haring and Ann Silver have been his favorite artists since he learned of their art. In 2003, he bought one piece of art by Silver which had an impact on his life. While he has never been a full-time artist, he has been a strong supporter of Deaf Art and Deaf artists.

This book project has been a wonderful experience because he has gotten to know Silver as a friend as well as an artist and has learned details of her life he would never have had a chance to know if not for this project.

Van Manen proudly lives downtown in two cities. He teaches in Chicago and does artwork in Seattle.

Author Acknowledgements and Thanks

First, thanks to Ann Silver for letting me write this book about her life and art. She recently said that she let me do this because I kept my eye on the prize and wouldn't let go. She's right. That's how things get done. Thanks for letting it happen.

Thanks too, to Jennifer Morrison for her editorial and publishing help as well as general moral support.

To the editors, copy editors, layout designers, and cover designers working in association with Empyreal Press, thanks for making this a beautiful book.

Thanks to Columbia College Chicago's ASL-English Interpretation Department where I teach, for the support and understanding of my fellow faculty. The chairperson recently told me to *Write On!* And to my friend and colleague Peter Cook, for knowing I could finish this book.

Thanks to students Erin Bullock, Alison Mlikan, Kate McAuluff, Celeste Peterson, Steve Saenz, Judi Stuber and staff Miss Nina Campbell, Lynn Cachey, and Lisa Butler who helped to make the *Ann Silver: ONE WAY, DEAF WAY - The Solo Show* in April 2012 a reality. They are wonderful people to work with.

And my thanks for the general support of Columbia College Chicago administrators and faculty. They all work to make it an amazing culture in which to teach and work.

Posthumously, thanks to my mother Janice Wilson and Silver's mother Belle Silver for all they did to bring us each to this place in life. They both would have loved reading this book.

Thanks to Norman Wilson, my stepfather, for always being in my corner with love and support.

And to Julius, Amanda, Erika, Justin and Allie, you have my love.

1140587R00106

Made in the USA
San Bernardino, CA
23 November 2012